The Complete Book

Upland Bird
Hunting

SHADY OAK PRESS

MINNETONKA, MINNESOTA

The Complete Book of

UPLAND BIRD HUNTING

Edited by Tom Carpenter

Tom Carpenter
Editor

Jen Weaverling
Production Editor

Heather Koshiol
Book Development Coordinator

Shari Gross, Kate Opseth
Book Production

Greg Schweiters
Cover Design

Laura Holle
Book Development Assistant

PHOTO CREDITS

Phil Aarrestad 13, 37 (bottom); **Joe Arnette** 50, 53, 54, 55, 56 (bottom); **Francis & Janice Bergquist** 9, 23*, 58, 82, 84 (left); **Greg Bergquist** 8 (both), 29 (top), 81; **Jim Levy/DenverBryan.com** 176; **Dave Budeau** 177; **Jim Casada** 5 (left), 24, 28, 32, 33 (top), 158, 160 (bottom); **Judd Cooney** 1 (top right), 6*, 7, 12, 18, 16, 45, 65 (bottom), 66, 67, 73, 76, 77 (bottom left & right), 80, 83 (bottom), 85 (right), 87 (top), 89 (top), 93, 98, 99, 100, 154, 155*, 156, 165 (left), 169 (both); **Richard Day/Daybreak Imagery** 140 (bottom right), 143, 144 (top), 147 (top); **Eric Hansen** 182, 183, 184; **Bill Hollister** 129 (top), 131 (left), 132, 135 (left); **Tom Huggler** 37 (top), 39, 41 (top), 43, 44 (bottom); **Tes Randle Jolly** 126, 129 (bottom), 131 (right), 133, 134 (top), 136, 137, 138 (right), 140 (left); **Don Jones** 1 (bottom right), 10, 14 (top), 19*, 22, 33 (bottom), 34, 35*, 36, 38, 44 (top), 61, 62, 65 (top), 69, 72, 74, 75, 79 (bottom left & right), 83 (top), 89, 90*, 92, 127, 128* (both), 130, 134 (bottom), 138 (left), 139, 141 (left), 163, 164, 165 (right), 168; **Mark Kayser** 91, 95 (top), 96, 103; **Dan Kennedy** 14 (bottom); **Steve Maslowski** 1 (left), 48, 49, 52, 142, 146 (bottom), 152 (left); **Patrick Meitin** 26, 173, 174 (bottom), 175; **Courtesy National Wild Turkey Federation** 151; 153 (bottom left); 147 (bottom), 153 (bottom right); **NAMG/Tom Carpenter** 40 (right), 42, 47, 146 (all top), 148, 149 (top), 150 (left), 152 (right), 153 (top); **Justin Robinson** 88 (left); **Ron Spomer** 104, 105, 106, 110, 111 (bottom), 116, 117, 123, 144 (bottom); **Jim Van Norman** 20 (bottom), 115, 135 (top); **Wayne van Zwoll** 178 (left), 186 (right); **Ben Williams** 4* (both), 5 (right), 11, 15, 17, 20 (top), 21*, 25, 27, 29 (bottom), 30, 31, 40 (left), 41 (bottom), 46, 51, 56 (top), 57, 60, 63 (both), 64, 68, 70, 71, 77 (top), 78, 79 (top), 85 (both), 86, 87 (bottom), 88 (right), 89 (bottom), 94, 95 (bottom), 97, 101, 102, 107, 108, 109, 111 (top), 112, 113, 114, 118, 119, 120, 121, 122, 124 (both), 125, 145, 149 (bottom), 150 (right), 157, 159, 160 (top), 161 (both), 162, 166, 167, 170 (both), 171, 172, 174 (top), 178 (right), 179, 180, 181, 185 (both), 186 (left), 187 (both); **Lovett Williams** 140 (top right), 141 (bottom). Asterisked (*) photos also appear on front or back cover.

Special thanks to Stephanie Crowder and the National Wild Turkey Federation.

MAP ILLUSTRATIONS

NAMG/Dave Schelitzche 53, 75. Remaining map illustrations: NAMG.

1 2 3 4 5 6 / 12 11 10 09 08 07

© 2007 North American Membership Group

ISBN: 978-1-58159-349-5

Distributed by:
Sterling Publishing Co., Inc.
387 Park Avenue South
New York, NY 10016-8810

For information about custom editions, special sales, premium and corporate purchases, please contact Sterling Special Sales Department at 800-805-5489 or specialsales@sterlingpub.com.

SHADY OAK PRESS

12301 Whitewater Drive
Minnetonka, MN 55343

Table of Contents

INTRODUCTION

The phrase "Going bird hunting" takes on different and wonderful meanings depending on where and when it is proclaimed.

In the South, in earliest September when it's really still summer out, bird hunting means dove hunting—a timeless tradition that takes place out on the on the edge of some sunflower field or pasture as the hot sun begins its afternoon descent and the birds start flying.

Later on, in November and beyond, bird hunting becomes bobwhite quail hunting across the South.

In the North, Northeast, and much of the East, bird hunting refers to ruffed grouse hunting, which is done in the thickest of thick places and requires the fastest of fast shooting skills. Once October hits full stride and the frost has knocked down a few of the blazing forest's leaves, woodcock flutter onto this bird-hunting scene.

Travel to the Midwest and out onto the Plains, and bird hunting is pheasant hunting—from the relatively simple roosters of opening day to the cagey, hard-running cocks of late season.

Continue westward and bird hunting becomes a hike for prairie grouse—sharptails mostly but prairie chickens too—out in the big grasslands that roll and stretch to every blue-skied horizon. You'll find Huns here as well, tough and welcome little imports that are incredibly fun to hunt.

Find yourself in the real West and, for at least a week or two a year, sage grouse hunting defines bird hunting. Keep climbing back or up into the badlands and rocks, and you'll find chukars—another great imported game bird, like the Hun and pheasant, that has filled an available habitat niche.

Hike up into the mountains, and bird hunting turns back to forests, where the elusive high-country blue grouse resides. You'll find surprising numbers of ruffs here too, wherever there's a little moisture to keep them happy.

Climb all the way to the spine of the Rockies—

or similarly, travel to the alpine tundra of Canada and Alaska—and bird hunting means ptarmigan chasing. You'll find spruce grouse in some of these wild boreal places too, where altitude or latitude keep civilization's encroachment at bay.

Head farther west and you're back in quail country, this time for lovely mountain and valley quail. Drop down to Arizona and New Mexico and you'll transition into the enchanting and starkly beautiful land of the desert quails—the Gambel's, Mearn's and scaled quail of December and beyond.

Somewhere in autumn's journey, fall turkey hunters get their chance at our biggest upland gamebird. And then of course there is spring turkey hunting—either the beginning or end of it all—at the calendar's other ebb.

If you're serious about your upland bird hunting, you know the addiction. If you occasionally hunt gamebirds, or are just starting out, you know the allure. *The Complete Book of Upland Bird Hunting* presents insights, strategies, techniques and tips—from a wide variety of hunters who

write, not writers who do a little bit of hunting—that will help you become an even better bird hunter no matter how much experience you have.

And the pages will make you want to expand your bird hunting horizons even further.

And therein lies what might be the only problem with the pages that follow. Somehow—through the words or pictures or a combination of both—you'll start to get hooked on yet another type of upland bird, and you will have to go hunt it in the magnificent place it calls home.

There's nothing wrong with that. In fact, it was part of the book's plan!

Tom

Tom Carpenter
Editor—Shady Oak Press

Chapter 1

PHEASANTS: MUCH MORE THAN AN AUTUMN STROLL

BY DICK STERNBERG

My ringneck addiction dates back to the time when a neighbor took me on my first pheasant hunting trip. I was 10 years old and too young to carry a shotgun, so I toted my trusty Red Rider BB gun. When that big rooster exploded from the grass right at my feet, I was so scared that I never even thought of shooting.

When the bird was well out of range, I finally took a shot and it folded. My neighbor's dog retrieved the bird and brought it back to him; then he came over and handed it to me. I guess I always knew that he really shot it, but I sure was proud.

Many other hunters hold pheasants in equally high esteem. According to the U.S. Fish and Wildlife Service, pheasants are the country's number-one upland game bird. In fact, wingshooters spend nearly as much time hunting pheasants as they do grouse, quail and partridge combined.

Why are pheasants so popular? It's the challenge. Not only are ringnecks maddingly clever

No other upland game bird compares with the ringneck for sheer, gaudy beauty. A citizen of places both wild and relatively tame (such as the harvested cornfield, above), he is an elusive, shifty and cunning runner ... and not at all easy to hunt after the season is an hour old.

when it comes to eluding hunters, they are quick to become "educated." In early season, the birds usually hold tight and you'll get plenty of close-range shots. But within a week or two, they've wised up and continue gaining experience on how to give you the slip. By late season, they're flushing out the end of the cover before you can stop your vehicle and get your gun loaded. A pheasant's cunning nature means you have to do everything just right or you'll go home with an empty game pouch.

The best pheasant hunting strategy depends on the situation. Working a big cornfield in early season is not the same as hunting a cattail slough as the season is winding down. But every good strategy has three elements in common: It minimizes the chances that the birds will detect your approach, it limits the number of escape routes for the birds, and it enables you to maximize your coverage of pheasant cover in the shortest time.

Understanding the Ring-Necked Pheasant

The introduction of the ring-necked pheasant to North America is one of the most successful game management stories in history. First planted in Oregon in 1882, these Chinese imports quickly gained a foothold and, within a decade, were a popular target of wingshooters. As the success story spread, the birds were stocked in other parts of the U.S. and Canada. Today, ringnecks are found in 39 states and 7 provinces.

Considering his show-off color scheme, it's a wonder that a ringneck rooster can hide so effectively. Nerves of steel—and strong legs—make the difference.

The popularity of this magnificent bird is easy to understand. When a gaudy rooster explodes from cover, even a dyed-in-the-wool wingshooter might lose his composure, allowing the bird to make a clean getaway. Many hunters consider pheasants the most wily and elusive of all game birds. Pheasants' first instincts are to sit tight or run rather than to fly, and they often slink away unnoticed in cover where it would seemingly be impossible to hide.

The sexes differ greatly in color and size, making the nearly universal "cocks only" hunting regulations possible.

Cocks measure 30 to 36 inches in length and weigh 2½ to 3 pounds. A rooster will have a conspicuous white ring around his neck, an iridescent greenish and purplish head, a red "wattle" around his eye, a dark reddish-copper breast, a powder-blue patch on his rump and a long, barred tail.

A hen pheasant is subtly beautiful in her own right, and masterful at hiding too.

A cock's leg has a spur that gets longer and sharper with age.

Hens measure 21 to 25 inches long—shorter than roosters, mainly because of their shorter tail—and weigh 1¾ to 2¼ pounds. A hen's back and sides are a mottled tan and dark brown; her undersides, a uniform tan. Hen's legs do not have spurs.

Pheasants thrive in areas with a good supply of small grains along with a mix of grasslands for nesting and heavy cover including cattail sloughs, riverbottoms, brushy draws, shelterbelts and woodlots.

Small grains—corn, soybeans, wheat, oats and milo—make up the bulk of the diet, but pheasants also eat a variety of weed seeds as well as grasshoppers and other insects. Because of their high protein content, insects are especially important to the chicks.

Like other game birds, pheasants have a gizzard to grind their food. To keep their gizzard supplied with fresh grit, the birds must pick up fine gravel in fields or along roadsides. This explains why you often see pheasants along gravel roads in the morning and evening.

Pheasants nest in practically any kind of

Birds that fly get cooked with cream of mushroom soup and eaten for Sunday dinner. Birds that run survive to make new runners. That's the breed of pheasant we hunt.

grassy cover including fallow fields, hay fields, roadside ditches, shelterbelts and railroad rights of way. In spring, the cocks scatter throughout the breeding grounds, crowing every few minutes to attract the hens. Once a hen comes close, the cock struts around her with feathers puffed out and wattles swollen to entice her to breed.

The hen selects a nesting site where the grass is at least 6 inches high, then she scrapes out a depression, lines it with feathers and leaves, and lays 6 to 15 brownish-colored eggs. The chicks hatch in 23 to 25 days.

The pheasant's polygamous breeding habits explain why "cocks only" hunting regulations work so well. Hunters can harvest more that 90 percent of the cocks in a given population, yet the few remaining cocks will breed with practically all of the hens. With most of the cocks removed from the population, the hens have less competition for winter food and cover, maximizing their over-winter survival and the subsequent production of chicks.

Pheasants rely mainly on excellent eyesight and hearing to elude predators—and hunters. But their sense of touch is also important. Their feet have pressure-sensitive pads, called Herbst's corpuscles, that help them detect vibrations produced by

approaching predators.

Pheasants are surprisingly short-lived. Their average life span is only 9 months, and seldom does more than 30 percent of the population survive to the second year of life. Pheasants more than two years old are extremely rare.

Pheasant range.

Pheasants want grass … and the thicker and taller, the better.

Pheasant Hunting Strategies

Following are pheasant hunting situations you will most likely encounter, along with some techniques for hunting each of them most effectively.

Hunting Grassy Cover

When looking for grassy cover, the standard wisdom is "the taller and thicker, the better." If the grass in one section of a large field is noticeably higher and denser, that's probably where you'll find the most birds. If a few trees grow among the grass, your odds improve even more; the trees give the birds a feeling of security. In a field where the grass is all of fairly uniform height, with no trees, you'll probably find more birds along the field edges than in the middle.

It's important to understand the daily movement schedule of pheasants using grassy cover. Some Conservation Reserve Program (CRP) and other grass fields have so much pheasant food, like grasshoppers and weed seeds, that the birds seldom have to leave. But most grass fields serve mainly as roosting or loafing cover. When the birds want to feed, they fly out to nearby crop fields in the morning and might not return until sunset. In some cases, however, they return to the grassy cover within a couple hours, loaf in midday, fly out to feed again in late afternoon and return to roost around sunset.

Hunt the grass right away in the morning. When the action slows, try an adjacent crop field. Then hit the grass again in late afternoon. But not all the birds do the same thing at the same time. The best grassy cover will hold a few birds at any time of the day.

Grassy cover is usually best in the early and middle part of the hunting season. Later, when snow mats down the grass, the birds are forced to seek heavier cover, such as brushy draws, shelterbelts, woodlots and cattail sloughs.

For a single hunter or pair of hunters with a good flushing dog, a big CRP field or other large expanse of weedy cover is surprisingly easy to hunt. Just start on the downwind side of the field and follow the dog. Don't tell the dog where to go; instead, let it quarter back and forth until it finds a scent trail.

Although some experienced pointing dogs work well in big grass fields, others have trouble pinning the birds down; while the dog is pointing, the bird is running ahead. A dog used for hunting grassy cover should be a good retriever. A wounded pheasant will often burrow into a clump of grass and the dog literally has to dig it out. Without a determined retriever, you could easily lose half the birds you drop.

A large group of hunters can work grassy cover by spreading out at 15- to 20-yard intervals and working the field in parallel strips. Blockers may or may not be needed, depending on the density of the cover. In heavy grass, the birds will most likely hold tight until the hunters reach the end of the field.

It's difficult for a single hunter without a dog to work a large grass field. The birds can easily scoot away in the thick cover, and the hunter never sees them. If you must hunt by yourself, the best strategy is to move slowly. Change directions often; left, right, zig, zag, even backtrack. Stop periodically to make the birds nervous. You may have to pause for 30 seconds or more; it sometimes takes that long to flush a skittish bird.

Hunting Rowcrop Fields

How you hunt a rowcrop field depends on how "dirty" it is. You can hunt a weedy cornfield the same way you would hunt a grass field. With the heavy ground cover, the birds are less inclined to start running as soon as they see or hear a hunter or dog. And the cornstalks in a dirty field are usually short, so when a bird flushes, you'll probably get a decent shot.

But hunting pheasants in a well-manicured cornfield with little grassy cover is another matter. Not only do the pheasants use the open rows as a racetrack, even the birds that do flush in range might be impossible to see with the giant stalks poking several feet above your head.

To hunt a big, clean cornfield successfully, you'll need a group of hunters. Starting at the downwind end of the field, the drivers should spread out 15 to 20 yards apart and walk up the rows toward the posters, who are blocking the end of the field. Ideally, the middle drivers should stay a little behind the outer drivers, funneling the birds toward the center of the driving line. Other hunters may walk ahead of the drivers along the field edges to keep birds from sneaking out the side, and to shoot at birds that flush well ahead of the drivers.

Although most hunters insist on using their dogs to hunt clean rowcrop fields, many veterans argue that a dog does more harm than good. Even an obedient flusher has a hard time resisting the urge to chase a rooster hotfooting it down an open corn row. Unless you have excellent control

Getting Started

*S*uccessful pheasant hunters get started well before opening day. They do some research to determine where pheasant populations are highest and then spend some time scouting for specific areas that hold good numbers of birds. And they contact landowners in pheasant hot spots and attempt to get permission to hunt.

Even if you have found a good pheasant area and gained permission to hunt, your preparations are still not done. Here are a few simple ways to improve your odds:

• Be sure to clean your gun. If you haven't touched it since last season, it could jam up on a critical shot.

• Brush up on your shooting by having a buddy toss some clay targets for you. Have your friend change position to vary the flight angles.

• Do a lot of walking to get in shape before the season starts. Wear your hunting boots to toughen up your feet—better to get the blisters before the season starts than on opening

To enjoy scenes like this, take some time to brush up on your shooting before the season, and also work your gear (and your rear) into shape.

day. Take your hunting dog on your preseason jaunts—dogs get out of shape too!

• Go through all your equipment—oil your boots, sew up that torn game bag or pants crotch, stock your shell box with a variety of loads, make sure you have all your choke tubes, and check to see that your gun-cleaning kit and first-aid kit are well supplied. Carry some first-aid supplies for your dog too—and don't forget water for you and your dog.

A farmer thinks it's ugly, but to a pheasant hunter this cornfield is lovely: grassy, weedy and full of places where pheasants can hide. For safety, let him clear the stalks before you shoot!

of your dog or are using a shock collar, leave the dog in your vehicle. If the dog gets away from you and the birds flush wild, nobody will get a shot. With the open cover, you should be able to find most of the birds you drop without a dog.

If you don't have a large group of hunters, look for smaller fields or those that have been cut into narrow strips. With a pair of hunters (one on each side), one poster and a good dog, you can move any pheasants within a strip and somebody is almost sure to get a shot. If you have no choice but to hunt large fields, work the outer edges and any adjacent grassy cover.

Hunting pheasants in a tall crop field or any other cover that is more than head high poses some real safety concerns. You might not be able to see drivers or posters within gun range, so never shoot at low-flying birds. Every hunter in the party should wear a blaze-orange cap for maximum visibility. Be especially careful when the line of drivers approaches the posters. The trapped birds often flush in unison and, in the excitement, inexperienced shooters may forget safety rules.

Picked cornfields and other rowcrop fields that have been harvested are usually overlooked by hunters. From a distance, it would seem that you could see any pheasants in these fields, but savvy hunters know that the birds can burrow under the stalk bases and hide in any remaining grassy cover when they're not feeding. Hunt these fields just as you would a grassland, letting your dog quarter in front of you and point or flush birds buried in the thick cover.

Hunting Wetlands

Wetlands with heavy growths of cattail, bulrush, horsetail, sedge or a variety of other marsh grasses hold some pheasants year-round. Birds often retreat to wetlands when they finish feeding, and the heavy cover furnishes shelter in stormy weather.

But the very best time to hunt wetlands is in late season when all the usual pheasant spots have been hunted to death and roosters are getting harder and harder to come by. Then, die-hard pheasant hunters know exactly what to do: head for the thickest "man-killer" swamps around. Not only do these dense wetlands provide excellent winter cover, they rarely see much hunting pressure. And in some heavily farmed areas, wetlands may be the only cover remaining after all the crops have been harvested and snow has matted down the grassy cover.

In early season, you may have to wear hip boots and slog through a foot of water and just as much mud to bag a pheasant.

But when the water freezes, hunting conditions improve. You should then be able to walk along the fringe of a wetland without falling through. And even if you do break through the ice, you'll only get your boots wet. Don't get brave and walk way out into the marsh; rarely will the ice there be safe. You're more likely to find birds along the fringes anyway, where the cover is thicker.

Trudging through dense cattails is real work. Sometimes the cover is so thick that you can barely move your legs. The trick is to look for deer trails where the vegetation has been matted down. Often, you'll find a network of trails that will allow you to hunt practically all of the marsh. Be sure to check any "islands" of higher ground within the marsh. Hunters often overlook these spots with grassy cover for loafing and roosting.

Without a good flusher/retriever, you have little chance of busting pheasants out of the nearly impenetrable cover, or retrieving any crippled birds. A wounded pheasant will slink away through the maze; only a powerful, determined retriever has much chance of tracking it down.

In late season, the birds often flush well ahead despite the dense cover. If you're hunting with a partner, you may be able to "pinch" the birds by splitting up and working the fringes of the marsh in opposite directions. This way, a bird flushed by one hunter might fly within shooting range of the other. For safety reasons, never shoot at any low-flying birds unless you can clearly see your partner.

Hunting Strip Cover

Practically every decent pheasant hunting area offers a network of "strip cover" that has the potential to produce pheasants. Besides road ditches and fencelines, other common types of strip cover include shelterbelts, farmhouse windbreaks, and the grassy fringes of railroad tracks, drainage ditches and streambeds. The best strip cover offers a mixture of tall grasses, brush and sometimes trees, and almost always abuts a crop field.

To hunt strip cover, start on the downwind end of the strip and slowly walk upwind, with one hunter on each side of the strip and a dog working in between. Try to keep the dog on the downwind edge of the strip so it can easily detect any

When the standard, easy spots quit producing—and they always do—it's time to head for the wetlands. You might get soaked and scratched, but the weight of a rooster or two in your game bag more than makes up for the price.

13

Hunting strip cover requires some strategy. Always work more or less into the wind. Try to keep your dog toward the downwind edge so she can scent what's hiding in the cover. Post a hunter at the far end. Put flankers off to the sides.

wind-blown scent. If your dog is hard to control and has a tendency to chase birds ahead of you, leave it in the vehicle. Otherwise, the birds will flush too far ahead and you won't get a shot. If there are other hunters in your party, post at least one of them at the opposite end of the strip. This reduces the odds that the birds will flush wildly and, even if they do, the poster may get a shot.

There's one drawback to hunting strip cover: When you get to the end of the strip, you may have no option but to backtrack to return to your vehicle. This is an inefficient use of your time, and there's little chance you'll flush any more birds on the return trip. So before beginning your hunt, study the area carefully and make a plan that will eliminate or at least minimize backtracking.

When hunting a railroad right-of-way, windbreak, road ditch or drainage ditch, there are two basic strategies.

If you're hunting alone, you can walk down one side of the tracks and walk back on the other. But try to keep your dog from crossing over the tracks and flushing birds that would otherwise hold until you walk back, giving you a better shot. The

same method works well for hunting parallel.

With a pair of hunters, you can "leapfrog" many types of strip cover, eliminating the need to backtrack. To leapfrog a railroad right-of-way, for instance, one hunter starts walking at the downwind end of a given stretch while the other drives around to the next crossroad, parks the vehicle and starts walking the next stretch. When the first hunter reaches the vehicle, he drives around to the next crossroad. You keep repeating this proce-

Typical road ditch strip cover. With a vehicle and a partner, "leapfrog" your way along (where legal).

14

dure until the entire stretch you want to hunt has been covered. Leapfrogging can be used to hunt any kind of strip cover, as long as there are roads or field access trails that allow you to drive your vehicle to crossing points.

If you're hunting with a partner but leapfrogging is not possible, you can minimize backtracking by working a piece of strip cover from opposite ends. If you're hunting a fence-line that runs across an entire section, for example, drop off your partner at one end, then drive back around and start hunting from the other end. When you meet in the middle, follow another piece of cover, like a shelterbelt, drainage ditch or corn strip, back in the general direction of your vehicle.

The biggest challenge of hunting strip cover is preventing the birds from flushing too far ahead. Don't try to chase them. Instead, stop. When you and your dog stop, the birds usually stop as well. Wait for your partner to swing wide of the strip, run ahead and block. If the birds are exceptionally wild, your partner might have to run several blocks to get ahead of the birds.

Shotguns & Loads for Pheasants

A ringneck is one of the toughest upland birds to kill. When you see a bird drop, you assume you made a good shot, but when you or your dog attempts a retrieve, the bird is gone. This explains why larger gauges, tighter chokes and bigger shot is necessary for ringnecks, when compared to many other upland birds.

You hear plenty of stories of kids gunning down pheasants with their .410s, and some experienced hunters swear by their 28 gauges. But most pheasant hunters use a 12 gauge to minimize crippling loss. A 20 gauge, however, will do the job under most conditions, with the possible exception of late-season hunting when the birds flush at long distances.

A modified choke is a good all-around choice for pheasant hunting, but in early season when the birds flush close, you might have better success with a cylinder or improved-cylinder choke. In late season, a full choke will extend your effective killing range. Some manufacturers offer "extra-full" choke tubes, giving you an even tighter pattern.

Ringnecks epitomize toughness. Use plenty of gun—usually a 12 gauge, but a 20 does fine under most conditions. Load up with high-power shells filled with No. 5 or 6 shot. You might even switch to 4s or 2s during the late season.

Standard loads of size 5 or 6 lead shot work well in most pheasant hunting situations, but many hunters switch to size 4 or even size 2 magnum loads in late season. If you'll be hunting pheasants on federal Waterfowl Production Areas or other areas managed primarily for waterfowl, steel shot is usually required. As a rule, use steel shot 2 sizes larger than you would if using lead. For example, if you normally shoot size 5 lead shot, you'll need size 3 steel.

Finding Ringnecks

Here are some prime ringneck locations. No matter where you hunt pheasants, you have to understand and read the habitat.

Retired Crop Fields

Fields enrolled in the Conservation Reserve Program (CRP) or other retired crop fields provide excellent nesting cover for ringnecks. Unlike hay fields, they will not be mowed during the breeding season, boosting the odds of survival for the young birds.

Cattail Marshes

The dense vegetation in these shallow wetlands makes ideal year-round cover for pheasants, but cattail marshes are especially important in winter when heavy snow mats down plants with weaker stems. The birds can move easily through tunnels in the vegetation, and they readily hear the rustling sound of approaching predators.

Shelterbelts

These rows of trees, planted as windbreaks to minimize soil erosion in open country, are highly beneficial to pheasants. They not only provide a refuge from winter blizzards, but the grass and brush along their fringes make good nesting, loafing, roosting and escape cover.

Drainage Ditches

In major agricultural areas, the dense grasses that grow along drainage ditches may be the only heavy cover for ringnecks. Most drainage ditches have sloping sides that offer refuge for the birds in windy weather.

Brushy Draws

In hilly country, brushy draws often hold large numbers of pheasants. Like drainage ditches, they offer the combination of heavy cover and a place to get out of the wind.

Fencelines

Wide, brushy fencelines, particularly those with some taller trees or bushes, almost always hold pheasants. The best fencelines are those adjacent to cornfields or other crop fields.

Terraces

These man-made, stair-step structures in crop fields are intended to minimize soil erosion. They usually have grassy cover that makes good loafing

An old homestead often provides an oasis of brushy cover and the tall, thick grass that pheasants love. Don't pass up these pheasant hunting jewels.

and roosting sites for pheasants that have been feeding in the fields.

Abandoned Farms

Old farmsteads that grow up to tall grasses and brush make ideal year-round pheasant cover. The birds use the undisturbed grassy cover for nesting, roosting and loafing, and the buildings and tree groves offer a windbreak. Abandoned farms are one of the first places to look for pheasants in winter.

Railroad Tracks

The dense cover that grows along many railroad rights-of-way may be your best hunting option in areas where it's difficult to gain access to private land. Unless the tracks are no longer in use and have been posted, they are usually open to public hunting.

Road Ditches

Roadsides that grow up to tall grass and brush usually hold a few pheasants, especially if they're alongside crop fields. The very best ditches have enough standing water to develop a good growth of cattails. Don't waste your time on ditches that have been mowed, burned or scraped.

Weedy Lakeshores

Often ignored by hunters, low-lying areas along shallow lakes commonly have dense stands of cattails or other wetland vegetation that hold surprising numbers of pheasants. Because of the standing water, however, you'll probably need hip boots to hunt here.

Brushy Streambanks

Stream corridors in agricultural areas usually have enough brushy or grassy cover to hold pheasants. If the streambed meanders a lot, however, you may have to cross the stream frequently to stay in the best cover. That means you'll have to hunt in rubber boots or waders—or just get wet.

"Dirty" Crop Fields

Crop fields that are not treated with herbicides often have a grassy undergrowth that holds pheasants. Rather than feeding in the fields and then retreating to adjacent grassy or brushy cover to loaf or roost, the birds just stay in the fields. Laid-back farming is a pheasant's best friend!

Never overlook harvested crop fields, or the fringes around them. This is especially true in the late season when pheasant food is in short supply and the waste grain makes for high-protein meals.

Nervous, suspicious, spooky and educated—doubled up—all describe late-season ringnecks. But the need for extra-heavy cover can concentrate the birds, making hunting more than worthwhile. Just don't go at the game like you did during Indian summer.

TIPS FOR LATE-SEASON RINGNECKS

As the pheasant season nears its end and snow covers the ground, you'll probably see more pheasants than you did in early season! It's not uncommon to find flocks of 50 or more birds in the vicinity of heavy cover like a woodlot, cattail marsh or brushy draw. Most of them will probably be hens, but there will be a few roosters as well. You won't find many pheasants in the grass fields and other light cover that held birds earlier in the year, because the vegetation has been matted down by snow.

But pheasants are notoriously hard to hunt in the snow. Even without snow cover, late-season birds are nervous and hard to approach; with snow, they're even spookier, meaning that you'll have to do everything just right in order to get close enough for a shot.

Here are some tips to help you shoot more late-season pheasants.

• Don't stop right next to a spot you want to hunt and slam your car door. Instead, park a block or two away and approach by sneaking.

• Don't hunt with a dog that requires constant verbal commands or a whistle. The noise will give the birds advance warning.

• If you're hunting with a partner, approach likely cover from opposite directions. This way, one of you could get a shot even if the birds flush prematurely.

• If there is fresh snow cover, look for tracks and scratchings. This way, you're pretty sure there are birds around the area, making it worthwhile to comb any nearby brush clumps or thickets thoroughly. Experienced hunters can differentiate the large tracks of a rooster from the smaller ones of a hen, making it possible to track the birds in fresh snow. It's not unusual to follow fresh tracks up to a clump of snow-covered brush, where you literally have to kick the bird out.

• As a rule, flushing dogs work better in heavy snow than pointers. A pheasant sitting tight in a snow-covered brush clump emits very little scent, but an aggressive flusher may stick its nose right into the clump and surprise the bird.

• Most late-season hunters prefer full chokes and few would consider using anything more open than a modified. Because many of your shots will be longer than normal, it's a good idea to use size 4 or 2 magnum loads.

CHALLENGES & REWARDS

Pheasants can at once be the most fun and maddening thing you ever hunted. Walk them up during the first hour or two of the season and you'll create some pleasant memories of good shooting and lovely Indian summer weather.

But then the pheasant hunting die-hards separate out from the autumn stroll-takers … and keep on hunting. Tough mid- and late-season birds require real hunting strategy. The flyers have gone to the big crockpot in the sky and only the cagey runners and hiders are left.

These are the birds that demand commitment—and strong legs—from both you and your dog.

But if you're up to the challenge, the rewards are worth every ounce of effort and every layer of leather that wears off your boots as you chase gaudy ringnecks across the land in hope of just one more heart-thumping and magical flush.

Finding Pheasants

Pheasants are definitely farm country birds. Good ringneck habitat consists of at least 50 percent crop fields, usually corn, soybeans, milo, sorghum or other small grains.

But crop fields alone will not sustain a good pheasant population. The birds also need adequate cover, usually in the form of undisturbed grasslands; brushy draws, fencelines, shelterbelts or ditches; wetlands; woodlots and thickets. Pheasants are surprisingly winter hardy, assuming they have good winter cover. This explains why their range extends into the prairie provinces of Canada.

Although pheasants are found as far south as Texas, the highest populations are in the North. South Dakota and Iowa are considered the top pheasant hunting states, but parts of North Dakota, Nebraska, Kansas and Montana are also known for their superb pheasant hunting.

Pheasants abound in many places, but you'll have to do a little homework to locate the best areas and find hunting access. It's worth the work.

Wild, Wild Western Pheasants
by Jim Van Norman

To hunt wild Western pheasants successfully you need to know their habitat, as well as a few specialized skills and tactics.

Western ringnecks have developed their own strategies for survival because of extreme pressure from predators, and the lack of extensive heavy cover. The cover well noted for pheasants on the Prairie and in the Midwest is nonexistent in most areas of the West. Pheasants use acute hearing and swift footwork to escape the reach of predators and hunters.

The traditional heavy cover recognized by most pheasant hunters—willow patches, briars, brambles, cornfields—is seldom present in the West. Tall, thick sagebrush, greasewood and weed patches offer cover to western pheasants. Greasewood especially provides excellent cover because of its thorny branches. It also produces a tiny seed the birds use as a food source. Keep in mind that these plant species seldom get larger

Many hunters think of the Midwest and the Plains when they think of pheasants. But some of the grandest adventures lie to the west, where the flush of a cackling ringneck is back-dropped by juniper-clad hills (or snow-capped mountains) and an endless, brooding sky.

Western pheasants love greasewood.

than three feet tall.

Creekbottoms, where short and tall varieties of grasses thrive, are also excellent habitat. Actually any cover, if food and water are within short flying distance, is a potential hiding spot for western ringnecks. There needn't be any grain crops nearby, either—weed and native grass seeds often suffice.

These birds have extremely sensitive hearing. Out here, a human voice will flush pheasants 200 yards away! Western ringnecks know that human voices mean major problems. So keep talking to a minimum, even to the point of working out hand signals between hunting partners. When handling your dog, use a whistle and electric collar to minimize the need for human voices.

Blocking, whether you have a dog or not, is essential when hunting a piece of cover. Blockers and a dog are highly recommended. Drive a vehicle into the area where the blockers are to be let out;

you'll spook fewer birds because they'll generally tolerate vehicles better than human figures moving about.

Ditch banks and fencerows are still common out West. Blocking is essential here too. Shelterbelts are, as always, excellent roosting areas for pheasants.

Cattail swamps, commonly referred to as thermal cover, are also widely used as roosting areas out here by pheasants. In fact, I love to sneak to a cattail swamp at first light and sit quietly until the roosters begin crowing. Morning crowing generally takes place as the sun begins peeking over the horizon and signals that the birds will begin flying or moving to their feeding areas. Either set up hunters to block these escape routes and send your toughest hunter and dog through the cattail tangle, or watch where the birds fly and take up hunting there.

Another common strategy we use out West is to carry a whistle that imitates a hawk. If you blow a hawk call once in a while as you traverse cover, pheasants will hunker down and sit tight, instead of running.

Another trick I use regularly is to vary my pace while walking though cover, stopping suddenly at irregular intervals. Coyotes and foxes, as they hunt, will stop momentarily when a bird is spotted hiding, then pounce. Ringnecks know this and will think they are spotted, then bust out and flush. Imitate that movement and you'll flush many birds that would have otherwise let you walk by.

Grass is critical habitat wherever pheasants live, and that includes the West.

Chapter 2

DOVES: FUN SHOOTING, SOCIAL TRADITION

BY JIM CASADA

Dove hunting is a low-key but high-enjoyment hunting adventure. Although not resplendently feathered, doves are still elegantly beautiful (far left). An airborne dove is a major wingshooting challenge. Another attraction: Doves thrive around agriculture (near left), which means dove hunting places are in ample supply.

For all-out fun, sporting camaraderie at its best and wing shooting at its most challenging, it is hard to beat a traditional mourning dove shoot of the "popcorn popper" sort. That's when the doves are flying so well and hunters shooting so frequently it sounds like kernels of popcorn bursting. Unlike most types of hunting, dove shoots lend themselves to group activity. And the fact that dove hunting is ideally suited for introducing youngsters to the shooting sports adds to the pastime's appeal.

While doves breed in all of the 48 contiguous states, with the majority of these states offering hunting, the sport enjoys the greatest popularity in the American South and Southwest.

Bird numbers, tradition and migration patterns explain this regional appeal. In Northern states, late August's first strong cold front usually sends the birds southward. Even in the South, inclement weather at the beginning of the season can wreak havoc with local populations. The only difference is that Southern hunters know they can expect replacement birds as migrants from the North arrive.

Indeed, from Virginia southward as far as Texas, devoted dove hunters enjoy not just Opening Day (almost always the Saturday prior to Labor Day) and Labor Day shoots. They manage fields carefully in order to enjoy sport for virtually all of September as well as shorter second and third segments of the season around Thanksgiving and Christmas.

In this part of the country, the key to having a plentitude of doves is ample food. Cornfields that have just been cut for silage, or newly harvested peanut fields, might provide a couple of barn buster shoots. Quite possibly the fastest action I've ever seen took place in a large watermelon patch that had just been bushhogged. For action spread over longer periods of time though, mixed succession crops such as browntop millet and sunflowers attract and keep birds best. This is especially true when strips are mowed every week or 10 days in order to put a new food supply on the ground where doves can feed.

THE ETHOS OF OPENING DAY

Dove hunting takes many forms. The traditional approach involves a large group of hunters and has some of the attributes of a country revival, with all-day singing and dinner on the grounds. This is particularly true of Opening Day. A glimpse at the first-day shoot I've participated in annually for two decades will give some insight on such events.

For the first week of dove season in South Carolina, where I live, hunting is allowed only in the afternoons. After that you can hunt all day. On Opening Day the crowd begins to gather at midmorning for the Turner hunt. The event, which will see 60 or 70 hunters taking to the field, combines family and friends with paying customers.

For weeks there will have been anxious phone calls of the "Have you got plenty of birds this year?" variety, and some hunters will even have done some scouting and picked out the spot for their "stand." For most though, the hunt is primarily a cause for socialization, relaxation and celebration. The smell of burnt gunpowder wafting across the sere September fields, where millet has recently been cut and baled, signals the start of another hunting season. Or, as a member of the host Turner family is fond of saying, "For me, it's Christmas in September."

Especially in the South, dove hunting can be a highly social affair with great food, great camaraderie … and an organized hunting plan that participants must adhere to.

24

Before the first hunter takes to the field or the first shot is fired, there are rituals to be followed. The master of the hunt will address the gathered assembly, reminding them that safety is of paramount importance, to avoid low shots, to be sure their guns are plugged and that they can expect a visit from the game warden sometime during the afternoon. Then it is time for a festive meal, which is in many ways as great a source of delight as the actual hunt.

The Feast

The evening before, a whole hog will have been placed on a huge barbecue grill, likely flanked by several hindquarters of venison and maybe some other delicacies. Slowly cooked and smoked for hours as flavors mix and mingle in a perfect culinary marriage, the meat will fall off the bone by mealtime.

Along with the featured fare will be all the bounty late summer country gardens can offer. There are juicy tomatoes, sliced cucumbers, pickles aplenty, fresh and preserved figs, fried okra and squash, probably a chicken or wild turkey bog (a rice-and-meat dish), all manner of vegetable casseroles, cantaloupes fresh from the vine, and slices of sugar-sweet watermelon so cold the rind instantly beads up with moisture.

For dessert there will be a belt-loosening array of delicacies—lemon and chocolate chess pies, maybe a cobbler or two with some hand-cranked ice cream, and if those in attendance are truly fortunate, possibly that most toothsome of delicacies, a scuppernong pie.

No one takes to the field hungry!

The Essence of the Hunt

Although the doves will not do a lot of flying until well on into the afternoon, anxious hunters nonetheless begin to filter to their allotted stands soon after lunch. There they will sit sweltering, possibly getting the odd shot, for two or three hours.

Around 4:00 p.m., it is as if the avian floodgates suddenly open. Doves are everywhere—singles, flights of three or four, and then a dozen or more at a time. The field rings with cries of "mark

In the late afternoon, the shooting (but not necessarily the hitting!) will pick up. Dove hunting is great for getting kids into the field.

right!" and "behind you" along with sounds of laughter and good-natured ribbing about easy shots that have been missed. Retrievers (of both the canine and youthful human variety) scramble after downed birds, and the shooting is virtually nonstop.

Within an hour or so things begin to slow, not so much for a lack of birds as because the better shots among the group have taken their limit of a dozen birds and have left the field. Others require more time, and there are always a few inept souls who fire three or four boxes of shells and have only a half dozen or so birds to show for their efforts. Eventually though, the fields empty and hunters wend their way back to the shady spots where they ate lunch.

Now is the time for the telling of tales—reliving hunts past, comparing this year to other years,

Understanding Doves

Doves feed on the ground, eating weed seeds of all kinds. That should give you an idea of where to hunt during morning and late afternoon feeding times.

Perhaps the first fact to emphasize about the mourning dove, biologically speaking, is the bird's incredible reproductive capacity. Its breeding season is one of the longest for any North American bird, and it reproduces successfully in all of the 48 contiguous states.

Together, males and females build the nests, which tend to be quite flimsy. The female lays a clutch of two eggs, and both parents share in the incubation duties, with incubation normally taking two weeks or slightly longer. The fledglings are ready to go on their own in 18 days. This means that on average, a pair of doves requires just more than a month to complete a nesting cycle, and one pair will typically complete several cycles in the course of a single year. Therein lies the explanation of why doves can, in suitable habitat, become so numerous!

Doves are exceptionally versatile when it comes to nesting habitat, but they breed most prolifically in the agricultural areas of the South, Southwest and Midwest. They are a migratory species, normally leaving areas of harsh weather just prior to its autumn arrival. This lets them avoid food shortages and the cold weather that affects their fleshy feet and ability to feed.

Doves are seed-eating ground feeders, with almost all of their diet comprising seeds or plant parts. Favorite foods include corn, smartweed, millet, sunflowers, ragweed, pokeberry and various types of pine seeds. Although the dove is the most harvested game bird in the United States, with more than 70 million shot annually, biologists note that other factors loom much larger in dove mortality: predation, diseases, parasites and pesticides to name the major ones.

= Summer and Fall
= All Year

Dove range.

bragging on a nifty double or the stellar performance of a new Lab, bemoaning inept marksmanship or congratulating a young hunter on his first doves.

Amidst this camaraderie hunters are breasting out the birds, wrapping them in bacon strips and maybe adding a jalapeño pepper or water chestnut and firing up the grill. Dogs tired from the heat and their labors will seek water, then shade. Someone will likely have had the foresight to cool a jug or two of homemade scuppernong or elderberry wine, and the delicate brew whets appetites for the feast of doves to come.

As dusk approaches, hunters young and old load up their dogs, stools, guns and other equipment and head homeward. Another Opening Day is done and another hunting season is well and truly begun. For some of those present, it will be their only hunt of the year. Others will return to the fields on Labor Day and many other times.

For everyone though, there's nothing like Opening Day. Shotshell manufacturers love it (nationally, estimates suggest one dove taken for every five to six shots fired), and in the world of the hunter it signals rebirth and renewal after many months of enforced inactivity.

EQUIPMENT FOR DOVE HUNTING

You can "get by" on a dove shoot, particularly early in the season when the birds haven't been pressured much, with nothing more than a gun, plenty of shells, and some camouflage or earth-tone attire. Serious dove shooters, however, pay considerably more attention to equipment and accessories, and they benefit accordingly in terms of better shooting, greater comfort and, at least arguably,

more enjoyable hunting.

Clothing needs can vary a great deal, thanks to temperatures that can range from the 90s on the first day of the season to wind-whipped 30s in early January. The primary things to keep in mind when it comes to attire are comfort and concealment.

Clothes should allow easy movement and mounting of the gun. A comfortable hunter is a more attentive one. Whatever the nature of the weather, try to wear clothes that blend in with your surroundings. A camouflage pattern with some green in it might be fine in the season's first segment, but you will want brown to be the predominant color on late-season hunts or when afield in arid regions.

Normally a comfortable pair of low-cut boots is what you want for footwear, but in muddy areas or fields intersected by drainage ditches you might find high-top rubber boots a plus. In Texas especially but also in some other southern dove hunting locales where rattlesnakes or cottonmouths can be a problem, snake chaps or snake boots might be advisable. If mosquitoes are plentiful, as is frequently the case for the September portion of

Early-season dove shoots can get mighty hot. A simple blind of camouflage material can keep you cool … and also hide you from sharp-eyed birds flying in.

Consider a stool of some type a necessity: It makes waiting for the birds a much more comfortable proposition. Pooch might even find a little shade beneath it.

the season, you will find either a "bug suit" of some type or plenty of repellant a necessity.

Finally, the real veterans of the dove shooting world use a couple of items of attire that deserve mention. A lightweight vest that does double duty as a shell pouch and game bag can be mighty handy and it is certainly better than scrambling to find more shells in a box or inside a stool. Also, especially in situations where doves are quite skittish, wearing a face mask will help keep birds from flaring (although I am convinced that movement, more than anything else, spooks doves).

While a stool might not offer the best shell storage (as has just been noted), a seat can add a great deal of comfort to the hunt. Stools come in a wide variety of forms, with those featuring a simple folding frame or the more common

padded seat atop a bucket. For shoots where there is at least a chance you will be afield for several hours, a stool with a backrest is a distinct advantage, and a seat that swivels is also appealing. Some of the nicer seats include a built-in Styrofoam cooler in which to hold water or soft drinks, something that is certainly welcome on hot days. Whatever its design, the stool should blend in with the surroundings.

Some hunters also carry portable blinds. These feature camouflage cloth attached to several stakes and can be erected with relatively little trouble. It is a good idea to carry a small hammer to drive the stakes into the ground, and the blind needs to be roomy enough for some movement (and to contain a dog if you hunt with one) and high enough so that it breaks all of your profile except your head once you are seated on a stool. Blinds are somewhat cumbersome and require a bit of time to erect and break down, but if you are hunting in a large field where there is little or no cover, they are a distinct advantage.

One final consideration when it comes to equipment is that of decoys. While dove decoys might not draw birds in quite the same fashion as a properly placed spread for ducks or geese, there is no question that they are useful. One common arrangement is a half dozen or so decoys placed on a telescoping metal pole with special arms to hold the decoys. Try to position yourself within easy gun range of this device. Alternatively, some hunters use a spincasting rod and literally cast decoys across power lines or the limbs of dead trees, both prime landing spots for doves. They then pull the monofilament tight to get the decoy into proper position.

TIPS, TACTICS & TECHNIQUES

Many dove hunters—indeed I would venture to say the vast majority of the breed—give little if any thought to approaches that will improve their effectiveness. They simply take to the field once or twice a season, sit where they wish or at the stand to which they are assigned, and have a jolly good time. There's nothing wrong with that, really. Dove hunting is about fun.

One scouting goal is to discover where the birds are feeding. Watering places are important too.

Scouting Is Key

Seasoned dove hunters, on the other hand, realize that there are rich rewards to be reaped from careful observation, pre-hunt scouting, and knowledge of typical dove behavior patterns. A good friend of mine, Rick Snipes, is a savvy student of the dove as well as one of those disgustingly talented wingshooters who regularly kills a limit with a box of shells ... with plenty of shells left for the next hunt.

Rick works at his dove hunting virtually year-round. This includes consultation on crop placement with the farmer from whom he leases, making sure that the food planted will hold birds throughout the entire time the birds can be hunted (portions of the period from early September until mid-January), and regular visits to the hunting area to see what the doves are doing. As a result, he knows when birds will likely show up, their favored flight patterns, which fields they are using the most, and the like. Knowledge of that sort can make a world of difference.

In arid areas like Texas and most of the West, doves are always attracted to ponds or stock tanks, and such locations can provide fast-paced shooting. The same holds true for roost areas if you happen to know where they are. (Over much of the South, clumps of cedar trees form a favorite roosting spot.)

Generally speaking though, most of your scouting and choice of a place to do your shooting will involve picking the right spot in a specific field. Where that is the case, keep the following factors in mind. Any (or all) information of this sort can put you in an ideal location while actually hunting.

• Doves love to light in a dead tree to survey the situation before flying into a field.

• Similarly, doves are drawn to power lines like a magnet, and at least one hunter I know has gone to the trouble of stringing a wire across a section of field for the sole purpose of giving doves a place to light!

• If a field where doves are feeding is surrounded by a treeline, as is often the case, doves will usually use a gap in the trees or a low spot in rolling terrain as an entrance point.

• By simple observation over two or three visits in the preseason, you can generally discern the doves' preferred travel routes.

Scouting also reveals dove roosting areas. Position yourself between this area and a feeding area for a late afternoon hunt.

Shotguns & Loads for Doves

Early in the season, and in particular on Opening Day, when doves are as close to being "low and slow" as the gray-winged speedsters ever get, any shotgun will work. Many hunters, especially on shoots where they know birds will be plentiful, opt for the greater sporting challenge afforded by 20 gauges or even a 28 gauge or .410. Still, most of the guns you see on the average dove shoot will be 12 gauges.

Double barrels, over-and-unders, semi-automatics (plugged, since you are only allowed three shells for this migratory bird), and pumps all have their advocates, and all work just fine. When the birds have not been hunted much, if at all, most shots will be at ranges of 25 to 30 yards, and skeet or cylinder chokes are the way to go. Similarly, size 7½ or 8 shot in light loads are all you need when the birds are close.

This changes, and dramatically so, as the first season progresses, and such is even more the case in the later seasons (usually around Thanksgiving and then at Christmas) when you deal with migratory birds that have been shot at a lot. Then shots suddenly stretch out to 40 yards or more, and the bigger, stronger birds might already have migrated many hundreds of miles and flown through their share of flak. That means tighter chokes are needed—modified or maybe even full—and you need a bit more reach out and "knock 'em down" power in your shells. High brass 7½s or even 6s are the way to go now, and a 12 gauge definitely becomes the gun of choice.

You see every style, grade and gauge of shotgun on a dove shoot, and the guy with the hundred-year-old Model 97 barn gun always outshoots the fancy boy with the Purdey. It's how you shoot those 7½s or 8s (in the early season) and 6s or 7½s (in the late season) that matters most.

You will miss doves. They're fast, erractic, unpredictable, misleading (and a lot of other adjectives!) all bundled up into one hard-to-hit flying dynamo.

HUNTING ALONE OR WITH A BUDDY

While most dove shoots involve a large number of hunters—anywhere from half a dozen to scores of them—it can also be a one- or two-person sport. The problem when hunting alone or with a buddy is keeping the birds moving. It is all too easy for the doves to light out of range, fly off when you move toward them, and then light safely again.

This challenge requires some "strategizing," as a good friend puts it. Sending a dog across a field can put birds aloft, or when hunting as a pair one hunter can move the doves while the second remains hidden and hopes for some shots. Mostly though, hunting of this sort requires careful selection of an ambush spot or some sneaky movement which leads to what is, in effect, jump-shooting—a shot or two at flushing birds. It's not classic dove hunting, but sometimes it's what you have to do.

MAKING SHOTS

If one distinguishing hallmark of veteran dove hunters is knowing how to pick a setup spot, another is the way they select their shots. Speaking through the sage insight of "The Old Man," in his book *The Old Man and the Boy*, Robert Ruark neatly summarized the essence of the matter: "Doves," the Old Man explained to his youthful understudy, "are the easiest hard shootin' in the world. Or maybe it's the other way around. Maybe they're the toughest easy shootin' in the world. I'm telling you right now, you figger to miss more'n you hit, and it would surprise me none if you didn't hit any for your first box of shells."

Typically, newcomers to the sport do a lot of missing (and even more muttering) until suddenly things like lead, swing and distance all fall together. Even then, finding the mark on a gray-winged speedster that dips, darts and dives can be

Don't budge, flinch or move as the dove comes in. When it's in range—and only then— mount your shotgun, find the target, swing through and shoot. You'll hit a few, but you'll collect more empties than birds on your stool at the end of the day.

if you keep getting tailfeathers, you can almost bet you are behind the bird and the edge of your pattern is catching the non-vital rear of the bird. Indeed, the vast majority of misses find the shooter behind the dove.

It's unlikely most hunters will ever approach anything close to hitting doves consistently. They are too elusive a target with too many imponderables to deal with—wind speed, sudden changes of direction, flaring and the like. Yet doves are incredibly plentiful over much of the country (not to mention the wing-shooter's Valhallas of Mexico and Argentina), with liberal daily limits and long seasons. Add to these considerations such factors as the wonderful eating doves provide, the opportunity for lots of action with family and friends, and the rush any shotgunner receives from "popping lots of caps," and you have some understanding of why, particularly in the Southern heartland, the arrival of dove season in early autumn is one of the high points of the year for hunters.

CANINE COMPANIONS

Dogs are by no means essential to successful dove hunting, but they can add appreciably to the overall experience. An obedient, sharp-eyed retriever with a good nose will add heft to your game bag, save precious time spent hunting downed doves when they are flying fast and furious, and help avoid the loss of game.

Almost any dog trained to retrieve can be effective on doves, although in my personal experience, Labs rank head and shoulders above other breeds. Boykin spaniels are quite popular where I live (they are South Carolina's state dog), but many of them are wound up as tight as a seven-day clock, thereby creating more problems than they solve. In fairness though, I have seen some stellar Boykins in the dove field, and a fine one is indeed a jewel.

Dogs require some special attention in the heat

devilishly difficult. However, keeping a few basic things in mind will help.

Don't budge, don't flinch, don't dare to move an inch until the dove is in range. Then mount the gun smoothly, find the target, swing through it and pull the trigger. The whole exercise should be almost instinctive, and the worst thing you can do is watch a dove flying your way, with gun at the ready, for 200 yards.

Most shots should be within 40 yards, and ideally they will be at 25 to 35 yards. Distance judgment is critical, and many misses are the product of nothing more than asking a gun to perform 60-yard shots.

It doesn't take a lot to bring a dove down, but

A good dog that minds and retrieves can make a dove hunt even more enjoyable. Take along plenty of water for him in the hot, early season.

of the early season, and it is best to carry plenty of water. Make sure your staunch companion gets plenty to drink, and it isn't a bad idea to pour cooling water over a dog once or twice in the

course of an afternoon.

One word of caution is in order when it comes to use of a dog: Nothing is less welcome on a dove shoot than a poorly trained retriever that runs hither and thither, blithely ignoring commands and treating every bird that falls as if it belongs to his master. Remember—this is a sport of etiquette, and your canine companions should show their manners too.

RELAXED TRADITION

Dove hunting might not offer the adventure of a bird hunting escapade to some far-flung place. The sport most often takes place close to home, but it's on turf that is very special to the hunter. And therein lies the attraction of dove hunting. It's a social affair. It's tradition. It's relaxed. It offers its own kind of excitement. It's a low-key and fun kind of hunting that every wing-shooter needs to experience.

Finding Doves

Finding doves can be relatively easy, when compared to the details of selecting a good stand and actually hitting the speedy fliers! Fields, trees and water are dove habitat's key components.

This land should be farmed to varying degrees of intensity: You want active fields as well as fallow meadows if possible. In the planted fields, corn, soybeans, oats, wheat, sunflower, milo and many other grains are key staples of the dove diet. Doves also love wild and abandoned fields with their wild crop of doveweed, foxtail, ragweed and myriad other weed seeds.

Find the right habitat and you'll find doves.

Trees are also important—to provide daytime loafing places as well as nighttime roosts. True forests aren't necessary, although they are often present. Fencelines, shelterbelts, treelines and tiny woodlots often provide all the trees that are needed.

Water is the final component of good dove habitat—preferably ponds, streams, wetlands or any other moisture with muddy margins where doves can land and get water. In the arid West, water is often a limiting factor, and an active windmill or full stock tank often makes the difference between having and not having doves in the area.

Chapter 3

RUFFED GROUSE: KING OF THE BRUSH

BY TOM HUGGLER

One spectacular fall, ruffed grouse were so plentiful in Michigan I was sure the "good old days" were back. My hourly flush rate, which I always combine with woodcock, was nearly 10 birds per hour.

During an afternoon jaunt in the Upper Peninsula while hunting behind my setter and short-hair, friends and I flushed 45 grouse in only three hours. The birds exploded from the young aspens in twos and threes, much like hen pheasants pressured at the end of a cornfield. "Incredible!" and "Unbelievable!" was how we described the experience that evening around our campfire.

For forty years I have hunted ruffed grouse all over North America. Believe me, that was as good as it gets.

Now flash back to an autumn five years earlier, when a friend and I were desperately trying to capture a flushing grouse on film for a videotape we were making. The few grouse we were able to find were so skittish we heard them but couldn't see them. By comparison, woodcock were much easier to target. If my memory is correct, we had

In many places, ruffed grouse populations follow cyclical peaks and lows; you have to know where and how to hunt for either scenario. Even where populations don't ebb and flow so much, finding birds is both art and science. Either way you're busting brush, and shooting at flying rockets.

16 woodcock flushes in the can before filming a single grouse. One grouse, a true survivor, ran more than 400 yards before taking to the air. "Incredible!" and "Unbelievable!" were again in the post-hunt campfire commentary.

I have seen population lows before. Believe me, that was as tough as it gets.

USING THE CYCLE TO YOUR ADVANTAGE

No one knows for sure why grouse numbers fluctuate so dramatically. Opinions—some ignorant, some informed—abound. Likely reasons are (1) lack of aspen buds (a prime food source) in winter; (2) not enough deep, fluffy snow for grouse to roost and thus escape predators; (3) too many goshawks or owls or coyotes or raccoons; (4) too much localized hunting pressure; (5) a cold, wet spring that kills young in the shell or chicks before they fledge; (6) a parasite that levels the population when numbers are high. Whatever is responsible, these cycles occur at roughly 10-year intervals, although research in Minnesota indicates minor upheavals every decade and major changes every 20 years or so.

Knowing where the cycle is helps me hunt grouse more effectively. Why? Because grouse act differently when they are plentiful versus when they are scarce.

Grouse Everywhere

In high population years, young grouse are always abundant. I can tell, not only at day's end from the tally on the combination whistle/counter I wear on a lanyard, but from the zany behavior of some birds. In that spectacular fall, for example, I witnessed two different grouse on separate occasions flush from the forest floor and fly a few feet to perch on a tree limb above my dogs. That behavior occurs so infrequently in heavily hunted states like Michigan, that I gawked back in disbelief. Another oddity: That autumn I watched birds fly right at me, and one nearly took off my hat.

Then, late one afternoon I was walking back to the truck with my shorthair at disobedient heel when she suddenly went on point in a ditch full of brome grass. Expecting a rabbit or pheasant, I was stunned when a grouse thundered out and made for the treeline 30 yards away. I shot that

bird, a young male. I assume he was either getting grit (the road was gravel) or was a fall-shuffle bird temporarily out of habitat.

Survivors

You get such "gift" grouse when numbers are high. But when populations are low, there are few, if any, young birds to pioneer new areas. Adults have had a year or more of experience dodging predators, and they are among the toughest of all upland birds to bag.

These grouse are already established in territories they know intimately. You don't surprise such "survivor" birds because they always know where you are and how to make their escape. A survivor grouse, like a gun-shy cock pheasant, sometimes runs ahead and flushes out of range. The survivor bird flies on silent wings to feed or roost.

Last November on the last day of hunting season, I was walking along the forested edge of a gravel pit when wings suddenly clattered next to my ear. A grouse (so close I could reach out and touch the trembling spruce bough it had abandoned) had waited until I was one step past his hiding spot before exiting. I like to think that wise bird will replenish the gene pool next spring.

I don't have any secrets for bagging such smart grouse, except to hunt slowly and deliberately, moving as quietly as possible, and hunting hungry with your gun up, index finger along the trigger guard and thumb on the safety. Savvy birds that know their home covers always manage to put trees between you when they flush. But every so often when one of my dogs has pointed a bird, I manage to pot it by quickly running around the balsam fir or clump of brush and catching it on the other side just as it rockets aloft.

I always think I'm so smart, until the next bird

When grouse are seemingly everywhere, some of them will do simple-minded things, like sit in a tree. It doesn't take much education to make the birds wary and skittish though.

To shoot grouse, you always need to be ready for the flush; ruffs seldom wait until you are ready and in perfect position, even when they're pinned in front of a pointer.

sense it's there without actually feeling it. The ability to recall experience causes me to look over grouse cover carefully before committing to an armed walk through it.

I believe it is also why my English setter often pauses to size up habitat. Sherlock, who may well be the best hunting partner I've ever had, appears to study the forest around him for a long moment before plunging ahead. So, what are we looking for?

Edges & Diversity

A grouse will live out its life in an area as small as 40 acres, if the habitat is prime. Typically, the area will be a mixture of forest types—mostly hardwoods with aspen preferred, but also containing birch, maple, oak, hickory, cherry and some evergreens such as balsam fir, spruce, hemlock or pine.

Such prime habitat contains "edges" made by logging trails, farm lanes, firebreaks, openings either natural or constructed, and what I call

bursts from cover the instant I turn my back on it. There are always cagey grouse out there. But each year I hope for a good hatch to put unsophisticated juveniles in the woods too.

PRIME HABITAT: WHAT TO LOOK FOR

Veteran hunters, relying on hundreds or thousands of memories, develop a sixth sense about where to find grouse. The mind of a seasoned hunter conjures an image similar to the habitat niche taking shape before him now, and—*bbrrrr*—a grouse suddenly goes up, almost as though on cue.

This phenomenon is similar to fishing, when the panfish angler knows when to wait for the bite and when to move on. The feeling is like a tingle of electric current so slight you

Prime grouse cover is invariably thick, with dense brush or saplings but a relatively "clean" (grass-free) forest floor. Openings are important for diversity and for creating the edges that grouse prefer.

Understanding Ruffed Grouse

Ruffed grouse are native to North America. Among the 11 known subspecies are both gray-phase and red-phase birds. Both sexes have neck ruffs and banded tails; however, in the male the ruff is more pronounced and the band is complete (the central tail feathers in the female typically have an incomplete or lighter-colored band). Males also exhibit a small orange-red eye comb if you look for it.

The polygamous males begin drumming on logs before daylight as early as March and as late as early June. Over several days hens lay an average of 11 eggs, which hatch in 23 or 24 days of around-the-clock incubation. If a predator destroys her nest, the hen will lay a second clutch of 7 or 8 eggs. Chicks stay with their mothers through the summer and begin to fly at about 2 weeks of age.

Depending on brood age, family units break up from late summer to late fall. Young birds move to new territories with both food and security; in particular, drummers (males) look for an area to claim and defend. Research by Michigan wildlife biologists suggests grouse might migrate up to 25 miles—an amazing feat when you consider that a typical flush is 50 yards or so—though most birds find good spots within a mile or two of where they were reared.

This movement is called the "fall shuffle," and it is a time of vulnerability. Young birds are often caught out of prime habitat, and they exhibit what some call "crazy flight" when they crash into living-room windows and show up in places they don't belong.

A school bus driver I know was challenged every morning one October when she turned around her bus on a wooded cul-de-sac. A grouse, black-feathered collar all erect, would make a daily run at her rig. Maybe the color yellow provokes a defending male; I know another story involving a road builder who had to shoo away a grouse from his yellow Caterpillar bulldozer day after day. One

In spring, a male ruffed grouse "drums" atop his territorial log, hoping to attract a hen to breed.

morning the grouse didn't show up. Had the bird moved on? Become a hawk snack? Or did a yellow-coated hunter add him to the game bag?

Whenever I flush a ruffed grouse, I ask myself many questions. What is that bird doing here? Is it moving to a new territory, or does it live here? Is it a young bird on the move, or an older bird already established? Alone or part of a family unit? What is it eating? Most important, how can I use this information to find another grouse?

Ruffed grouse range.

"compromises"—where one type of cover blends into another. Examples include a corridor of brush separating woods from fields or a wet stream bottom of ponderous black oak or sycamore that grades into a beech upland. These edges might run for hundreds of yards—an aspen clearcut, for example, next to a cedar swamp—or they can be as brief as a patch of gray dogwood around a gone-to-seed apple tree.

Differing habitat ages contribute to diversity too. By itself, an old-growth forest doesn't help grouse because the crowns of mature trees create an umbrella-like canopy. This canopy prevents sunlight from reaching the forest floor and producing some of the foods that grouse love—wintergreen berries, clover, wildflower petals and other ground covers—along with an understory of shrubs and fruits such as grapevines, rose hips, blackberries, witch hazel, wild currant and dogwood.

The reason Minnesota, Wisconsin and Michigan produce the nation's best grouse hunting is because aspen is a key timber resource in the Great Lakes region. Grouse use aspen of all ages. Cocks set up mating rituals on drumming logs surrounded by heavy stem density, which occurs within a couple years after aspen is cut (the aspen roots send out suckers that "explode" with new growth within two months of the timber harvest). Hens often lay their eggs at the base of a mature tree spared within an aspen clear-cut. The heavy stem density protects adult breeders from predators. Ground cover appears along with bracken fern and an understory of berry canes and fruiting shrubs.

One of my favorite places to hunt is a 10- to 20-year-old aspen stand because it is nearly always full of grouse food and yet continues to afford security to the birds. As the aspen ages, it becomes more important as a winter food source of buds

Two key words describe good grouse habitat: young and diverse. Look at the brush, aspens, conifers and clover mixing in this habitat, not to mention a logging-trail opening to break things up. These hunters, and their dog, will be venturing into the real cover to find the birds.

No matter where you hunt grouse, edges are key—the seams between one cover type and another (shown here), as well as the interface between open areas and cover. Hunt these places and you'll narrow your miles-walked-per-flush ratio.

and catkins.

But grouse also thrive in low-aspen habitats such as the birch-maple forests of New England, the oak-hickory forests of the Appalachians and other states to the south and west. These forests typically contain a mixture of conifers, ground covers and shrub understories. But logging, fire, wind and any other element that changes the forest, encouraging old trees to tumble down and new plant life to grow, will benefit grouse. In short, no matter where you hunt, give a grouse diversity and he'll find a home.

FOOD SOURCES: THE LEAST FACTOR

In researching for my book *Grouse of North America*, I learned that ruffed grouse eat more than 100 kinds of food. They love mushrooms, will swallow whole acorns and beechnuts, and will even eat toxic foods such as mountain laurel, nightshade berries, poison sumac buds and poison ivy leaves and berries. I have found burdock and cockleburs in their crops.

From the vantage of a treestand where I was deer hunting with a bow, I once watched three grouse fly into the branches of a freshly downed aspen and ravenously rip away buds at the rate of one per second. They ate hundreds.

Grouse are opportunistic, their diets changing with whatever is available. Chicks, for example, need protein and a hen mother makes sure her charges get protein by leading them to ants, grasshoppers, beetles and other insects.

Early in the hunting season, many of the crops of birds I open contain insects along with green matter such as strawberry leaves and clover leaves. As the season progresses, I find acorns and other mast, along with mushrooms, berries and fruits. When the season winds down in December, grouse show a marked preference for buds, catkins and hardy ground cover foods like wintergreen berries and rose hips.

This grouse was feasting on gray dogwood berries. Guess where you'll want to hunt.

One time I broke open the crop of a bird I killed in early November and was surprised to find several whole beechnuts. After a bit, I remembered a small beech forest on the other side of a stream. Arriving there, I shot two of several other birds I flushed that morning.

Although the forest is a smorgasbord in fall, grouse often prefer a certain food that is suddenly available. I call it the "least factor." It is similar to the bowl of tiger shrimp that disappears soon after someone puts it on the restaurant buffet table. Although most grouse crops contain a variety of

These ripe highbush cranberries will hold grouse in the vicinity. Identify preferred grouse foods where you hunt, then frequent those areas.

food types, you may well notice a certain kind to be more abundant. Find that food source and you will find the birds. Examples are mushrooms (check out that shaded section of woods), grasshoppers (try the brushy edge next to the alfalfa field), grapes (that old fence row with the grapevine tangles) and dogwood berries (take a stroll along that clear-cut edge where the bushes are thriving).

The key to maximizing your time and energy is to learn where grouse will be and when. Food sources are important early and late in the day, but where do birds go at other times?

Young-of-the-year birds looking for home territories to claim can be just about anywhere. Even so, grouse always require covers as secure as they can find, and that includes mature birds who stay home. They, too, are challenged by an ever-changing world. As bracken fern withers, leaves spiral to ground and annual vegetation goes rank, grouse become more vulnerable to hawks, owls and two-legged predators. For this reason, they move into covers more secure as autumn, and the hunting season, progress.

Birds I find in September among the aspen swells and stands of ridge oak shift to mixed hardwoods and conifers by Halloween. By Thanksgiving Day, they are typically in heavier covers, yet not surprisingly these include the last-to-freeze lowlands, stream-bottom brush and swamp edges. Aspen/alder compromises are key places to check out then. So are ground-hugging conifers seamed with aspen, birch and other hardwoods.

HUNTING THE MICROCOSM

You can apply the least factor of food to other kinds of habitat that grouse use. Put another way, the panoramic view of grouse woods may look alike to the inexperienced eye, but grouse won't use all of the cover at once. You must train yourself to look for the microcosm within the big picture. That clump of red osier dogwood among the swamp-edge blowdowns may hold the only grouse in this patch of cover. That is why you should check that black spruce next to the birch clump. And that seam of goldenrod tucked among the cherry-red crabapples.

Get the picture? Now, why are grouse likely to be in those places? Because they are the thickest and therefore safest spots for birds to hide.

Early in the season, hunt in the hardwoods. Once there, spend your time finding "microcosms"—the thickest and safest spots where grouse like to spend their time.

Another way I look at grouse habitat has to do with the "green factor." If early season grouse use a habitat mix that is 75 percent hardwoods and 25 percent conifers, by December the mixture is closer to 50/50 and in the dead of winter can tip to 75/25. The cloaking boughs of spruce, pine and other evergreens help hide birds from raptors, and the cover affords warmth on cold winter nights when there is not enough fluffy snow to provide snow roosts. I assume it is for reasons of warmth and security that grouse often band together in winter. The scarcity of preferred food may also be responsible.

So, to find grouse throughout the long hunting season, think food and think security. These are the keys you always need to consider.

DOG POWER

You don't need a dog to hunt grouse successfully if you (1) hunt with purpose in the places I have outlined, (2) hunt "ready" as much as possible, (3) do not take your eye off hit birds until you can hang your hat as a marker on a limb where the bird fell. A friend of mine, who passed away a few years ago, shot more than 600 grouse over a 30-year hunting career in upper New York State. He never used a dog and claimed he never lost a grouse.

Knowing that, though, I would not hunt grouse with the same passion were it not for my dogs. They add the prologue and epilogue to what I consider to be high drama indeed. They share my pleasure, and they furnish warm ears to stroke

Shotguns & Loads for Grouse

Carrying a gun that fits you and that you feel confident shooting is the first step toward becoming a successful grouse hunter. A double gun is the perfect firearm because it is rare when more than two shots can occur. I shoot both an over-and-under Winchester 101 with 28-inch barrels and an AyA No. 2 side-by-side with 29-inch barrels. Both guns fit me like a tailored suit, and I have no preference of one over the other.

I like my six-pound 28 gauge guns because they are relatively light. I don't need a 20, 16 or 12 gauge because most shots are only 25 to 30 yards, and yet I have killing power for targets to 35 and even 40 yards when I use a No. 6 or No. 7½ field load. Typically, though, I drop a No. 8 or 8½ into the first barrel because I hunt woodcock in the same habitat as grouse and because—in the early season at least—I need a dense pattern to strain shot through leafy canopies. When the woodcock are gone, I switch to the larger (No. 6 or 7½) pellets for better penetration and downrange lethality.

Open chokes and No. 7½ shot are perfect for grouse, though you might tighten up the choke a little (no more than modified) and go to 6s when some leaves come down and your shots start stretching out.

Use open chokes (skeet or improved cylinder) as long as leaves are on the trees. When the canopies come down, switch to improved cylinder and modified. When grouse flush wild, typically on windy days, I'll screw a full-choke tube in my second barrel.

OTHER GROUSE FACTORS

You can learn a lot about grouse by tracking them in snow. Grouse walk greater distances than they fly, and their tracks tell good stories. You will learn what they eat, where they roost and how they use habitat. You might even get close enough to flush the bird, if the track is fresh and the snow is new. Some grouse apparently feel safe after a first snowfall and will hold better for dog or hunter. (If the bird has an Achilles heel, this could be it.)

Days of sleet or rain typically drive birds to the conifers where they wait out the storm. I have learned that grouse spend more time feeding during days of impending bad weather. On cold or wet mornings, they often stay in the roost until well past daylight. They grow hair-trigger nervous on windy days when you might hear a dozen drumbeat flushes before spotting your first bird. On bitter-cold days they feed late in the afternoon and go to roost early.

For the author, the companionship and hunting efficiency of a good dog combine to make grouse hunting all the more special. "Good dog" is the key idea. Leave wide-ranging, disobedient canines at home, unless you're more interested in a stroll than shooting a brace of ruffs.

SHOOTING A DOUBLE

Odd perhaps that I've shot doubles on woodcock, several species of quail, pheasants, Hungarian partridge, prairie chickens and sharp-tailed grouse. But I have never shot a true double on ruffed grouse.

A true double is when a pair or more birds ignite at once, and you kill two grouse with two shots. I can think of at least two times when I missed with the first tube of my two-barreled gun, killed the bird with my second shot, and then followed the escapee with an empty gun.

Even when I know it's coming, the roar of grouse wings always unhinges this hunter. In my

when I relive the day's highlights before a cabin fire at night. The hunt just wouldn't be the same.

I have hunted grouse behind many kinds of dogs, both flushers and pointers, and while I prefer pointing breeds for grouse, the decision is a very personal one. Whatever the breed, the dog must hunt for you. Incorrigible dogs that won't come when called, insist on hunting in the next township, bite grouse in two, chase deer and otherwise behave shabbily should be left home or given away.

mind's eye I know grouse are so deft at dodging stuff, including my shot pattern, that they hold the cards, not I. The instant knowledge of two birds in the air sluices my brain with adrenaline and the certain knowledge that I have blown this chance before. Maybe I subconsciously flinch, afraid to have two birds down in heavy woods and facing the horrible prospect of losing one or the other or both. And so I miss, chuckle to myself and reload my gun.

And then I tip my hat to the royal ruffed grouse, cherish the single bird my dog retrieves and we move on to new adventures. That's grouse hunting, and that's what I live for.

In many ways the ruffed grouse (above) represents game bird royalty. He takes you to beautiful places, makes every hunt a challenge, and isn't easily hit with a string of shot. But every once in a while the cosmos comes into balance and a bird tumbles from the sky for you (right). These are moments to be cherished and remembered, out there amongst autumn's glory. Just being there is enough. A grouse in hand is a bonus of the best kind.

44

Finding Ruffed Grouse

*R*uffed grouse are native to 40 states and have been introduced to Nevada, Colorado and Oklahoma. States without these noble birds include Florida, Mississippi, Louisiana, Texas, New Mexico, Arizona and Hawaii. Ruffed grouse also live throughout Canada.

The best grouse hunting region is the Upper Great Lakes, where respective annual harvests in Minnesota, Michigan, Wisconsin and Ontario range from one-half million to one million birds. The New England and Middle Atlantic states are also home to good numbers of grouse along with Pennsylvania and New York. Fewer birds occur as one travels south of the Ohio River Valley and the Great Lakes. Limited hunting opportunities occur in Georgia, Kentucky, the Carolinas, Indiana, Missouri and Iowa.

Hunting improves in the Pacific Northwest, most notably in Washington and Oregon. Montana, Wyoming, Nevada, Utah, Idaho and North Dakota host hunting seasons, and the grouse chasing can be very good in some locales.

And believe it or not, ruffed grouse truly are a common man's game bird. Despite all the romantic old-time literature touting expensive double guns and secret coverts, some of the best hunting can be had with any old open-choked shotgun in your hands and a pair of good boots on your feet, right on public land. In fact, as long as logging and clearcutting occur rotationally on national forests, state forests, county tax-forfeited lands and other publicly owned backwoods places that grouse frequent, hunting should be great and affordable.

For the absolute best grouse hunting, you'll probably have to bust brush in Minnesota, Wisconsin, Michigan or Ontario. Pockets in the Rockies hold good numbers of birds, as do places with the proper habitat in the Appalachian states.

Dogless Grousing — Going It Alone
by Tom Carpenter

You too may dream of the day when you will have enough time to properly train and hunt with a good ruffed grouse dog. I do.

But a growing family and many other hunting pursuits usurp any available canine training time there might be in today's busy life. I suspect I'm not alone in this camp. Plus, I'd feel guilty if I didn't chase birds with the mutt every precious hunting minute I had in a fall.

The truth is that you don't need a dog to hunt ruffed grouse. In fact, an improperly trained or unruly dog is a huge handicap in the thick and unforgiving places grouse call home.

Okay I'll admit the whole truth. I love hunting grouse without a dog. All alone. Just me and a shotgun and the strategies and techniques I've learned over a couple decades of skulking through the pop-

ple brush, tag alders, witch hazel, dogwood and raspberry canes from September through December.

To start, know where grouse like to be. Find those seams and edges—between aspen and tag alders, aspen and spruce, mature timber and brush, brush and field, any opening and cover. Find the thickest and brushiest (but not grassy) places. Look for wet spots—marsh edges, creekbottoms, wet gullies, spring seeps—because moist places offer both thick vegetation for grouse to hide in and good food for grouse to eat.

Sneak along slowly. Although my pace isn't as dreadfully slow as I go when still-hunting a deer, I still sneak along. Calmly. Quietly. Gun ready at all times.

Weave in and out of the brush. Stop often and look. Wait a little bit. Listen for the "peeping" that

When grouse hunting alone, stick to the seams and edges.

a nervous grouse makes. Be ready. Listen for a grouse walking ahead of you. You can do all this *hunting* when you sneak slowly and quietly. Let your feet take you where it just looks grousy.

If you flush a grouse and miss or don't get a shot, follow up in the direction the bird went, to attempt a re-flush. I believe half of all grouse fly off on a straight line. The other half veer off. So if you don't actually see the bird veer off, follow straight-on in the direction it went. If you go a hundred yards and don't get the re-flush, start circling and wandering around.

I have flushed the same bird 7 times this way, taking the 50/50 chance that it went straight, and then clover-leafing around if I passed where I thought it should have landed. (To answer your question—yes, the 7-flush bird won every round!)

First shots are often the best shots though, when everything's instinctive and reactive and you just up-and-shoot. That's why hunting alone is good. Without a partner's whereabouts to worry about, you can swing and pull the trigger without hesitation. That's how you hit grouse. I never think about how I made any grouse shot; I'm just thankful I did!

If you hit the grouse, watch where it thumps the ground. Walk to that spot directly without taking your eyes off it. Hang your orange hat when you feel right. Stop. Stand there for one, two, three minutes, and just look. I find 70% of my grouse this way, somewhere within my field of vision.

If the bird is fluttering in the leaves in its phantom death flight, your job is even easier. If you don't see the bird after stopping and looking, make circles, spiraling outward two feet at a time, searching. It's painstaking but it works.

I have never lost a bird that I hit and saw fall, using these methods. If you think your shot might have been good but you didn't see the bird tumble, then you owe it to the game to go look.

A trio of grouse taken on two feet, without any four-legged assistants.

If you think, walk and look after the shot—and never shoot a double when you're hunting sans dog—you will find every bird you drop.

I love hunting grouse this way, all alone with just the wind fluttering the last few yellow popple leaves against an October blue sky as I weave in and out of grousy looking spots, smelling and feeling autumn's magnificence in the air. It's about as free as you can be.

And every once in a while a grouse will thunder forth from the brush, my shot string will meet it out there in a magical way I don't want to analyze, and I will jog over to pick up the bird. Burying my nose in the grouse's breast feathers for a full and wonderful whiff, I always think:

How did I get so lucky?

Chapter 4

WOODCOCK: A FINE FISTFUL OF FEATHERS

BY JOE ARNETTE

I am perched on the iron-cold tailgate of my truck. My springer spaniel sits beside me, shivering lightly and winding messages on thin fingers of breeze. I wonder if his butt is as chilled as mine or if his tremblings are from nervous anticipation. The dog is a seven-year veteran of mornings like this one. He knows the ropes and sits with restrained impatience, ready to play a familiar role leading to a familiar end—the deceptive, helicoptering flush of woodcock.

But there is time enough, so the dog and I wait. Stay with us, and let's talk about woodcock.

No doubt woodcock are very "different" from your standard game bird (far left), but they're also very special. From the tips of their long beaks to their perfectly camouflaged russet plumage to their little fan tails (left), woodcock make for a fine hunting celebration out there in the thickets, field edges and bottomlands of autumn.

HOOKED ON WOODCOCK

Woodcock are hunter-friendly. They don't demand that I get on their trail at the first hint of dawn. Yet there is something about the birds—where they live, and the potential in an October morning—that compels me to arrive early on

their turf to sit with a cold rear and a warm heart, with an arm around a dog under a new sun igniting an autumn day. Woodcock do that to me.

I shot my first woodcock as a shirttail kid in stunning cover, with a decent gun, over a fine dog. Since that long-past morning, I have hunted these birds on a good chunk of their range behind a dozen breeds of gun dogs. I thrive in cover where woodcock live because they are there.

49

Look for woodcock in thick cover, often the same types of places you'll find ruffed grouse. But because woodcock probe the ground for earthworms, look for moist areas with soft soil.

I admire dogs that hunt woodcock well, shotguns that rise easily to the flush and people who own the dogs, raise the guns and treasure the birds. I admit to a love affair with all things woodcock. To me, they are a passion unlike other passions, because they are a bird unlike other birds.

A UNIQUE UPLAND GAME BIRD

Imagine, for a moment, that we are designing a complete upland game bird. We'd want a unique bird that flies against ideas of what is typical; a gypsy loner that moves with the seasons but drops into predictable habitat and stays a while. Let's say we fancy smooth-handling guns, light loads and wing shooting in thick cover over close-working dogs. Our ideal bird must hold well for the dogs, then flush fast and fly like a scatterbrained bat. Taken together, that is a lot to ask for in our design. But we need not waste our time; nature has already invented the American woodcock.

Where Woodcock Live

Woodcock occupy the entire eastern half of North America from Canada's maritime provinces south along the Atlantic Coast to central Florida, westward into east Texas, then north in a nearly straight line to the southeastern corner of Manitoba. Discounting occurrences in odd locations, the range of the woodcock has not changed substantially for centuries. They are not birds of deserts, high prairies or mountains, which means you won't find many of them too far west of their Texas-to-Canada boundary line.

Because woodcock are both reasonably widespread and migratory, biologists charged with their management divide the birds into two subpopulations roughly separated by the Appalachian Mountains. Although there is overlap on their deep south wintering grounds, the populations are managed as separate groups of birds occupying discrete regions—the Eastern and

Central—conforming to waterfowl's Atlantic and Mississippi Flyways.

Where to Find Woodcock

Wherever they live, woodcock require specialized woodland habitat. Don't look for them in mature timber. Woodcock favor moist soil in second-growth hardwoods broken up with scattered openings or fields. These birds need young, vigorously growing habitat like 10- to 15-year-old clear-cuts, burned-over forests or abandoned farms—all of which signals that top woodcock cover is temporary, averaging 20 to 25 years. At its peak, one of my favorite covers, for example, could produce 20 flushes an hour, but now it has aged and rarely holds more than a bird or two.

"Hunt the alders," say woodcock veterans. Like many old saws, this one has truth to it. Woodcock regularly use stands of alders with strong vertical growth and high stem density as both feeding and daytime resting cover, especially during early fall when leaf thickness ensures cool, damp earth harboring plenty of worms. But alders aren't the whole show; in fact, they become less productive as autumn advances.

Arguably, the best Northern cover is made up of a medley of young hardwoods—such as aspen, willow and birch—fringed by alders and scattered with low pines, briars and brambles. Such cover can hold a lot of birds, particularly when it is pioneering fertile pastureland or abandoned orchards. (Never bypass clusters of old apple trees; they are enduring cover.)

Whatever the specific habitat, woodcock prefer relatively open earth uncluttered by grass or thick ground cover beneath a low tree canopy.

North to south, woodcock have special needs, and frequent cover types that are similar in char-

You won't find woodcock in mature timber. Instead, look for them in young, second-growth forest like this. Openings are important for the diversity and thick edges they add to the cover. Once in the thick of things, concentrate on tag alder edges and other areas with moist soil where woodcock bills can probe for worms.

acteristics like age, canopy height and understory. That cover may be mixed hardwoods in the North or, in the South, cypress bottoms, stunted hardwoods and pines, clear-cuts and burns. But across the board woodcock coverts share many basic features: young forest, damp areas, openings.

Woodcock Are Hunters' Birds

Woodcock are often labeled second-class targets of opportunity for ruffed grouse and quail hunters. But overshadowed as they sometimes are

Understanding Woodcock

With super-sized eyeballs, an upside down brain and a long, probing bill, a woodcock is an odd (but perfectly camouflaged) package.

Woodcock are relatives of shorebirds. Eons ago, woodcock forebears gave up communal life at the water's edge and began an evolutionary trek to a solitary, low-profile existence in the uplands.

Woodcock bills pushed out inches for capturing worms that can make up over 80 percent of their diet. These probing bills evolved grasping tips laced with nerve-endings for pinpointing their beloved worms inches below the earth's surface. Woodcock eyes became disproportionately large and moved high and far back on the skull, which gives woodcock an extraordinary field of vision front, rear and skyward. To accommodate these super-sized eyeballs, nature flipped the woodcock's brain upside down and repositioned the ears below and in front of their eyes.

When woodcock finished their move to the uplands, they had given up running for sit-tight tactics; traded shore colors for browns of the forest floor; and opted for plump bodies, stubbed tails and broad wings to accommodate tricky flushes and oddball flights through uncivil cover. The illogical but very special result of a million years of Darwinian fine-tuning is the American woodcock.

Male and female woodcock are colored alike, but there sexual similarity ends. Adult hen woodcock bodies average about 20 percent larger than males, though differences aren't always clear cut. However, birds in good condition that weigh between 7 and 8 ounces are virtually always females, while those scaling in at 6 ounces or less tend to be males.

A misconception is that bigger woodcock are always migrating flight birds and the smaller ones are resident birds that have yet to begin migration. Not so. The larger birds are females.

Other than obvious body size differences, bill length is a quick way to sex birds in the field. Although there is overlap, a bill close to or longer than 2¾ inches signals a female; a bill 2½ inches or shorter tags the bird as a male. For easy in-the-field measuring, just break out a dollar bill and lay the bird's beak across it; a dollar bill is 2½ inches wide.

Research indicates that woodcock numbers are closely related to four types of critical habitat: clearings for male courtship displays during spring; young hardwood stands for nesting and brood rearing; fields for roosting; and dense alders or early-growth hardwoods on poorly drained, worm-laden soil for resting and feeding. Although the last cover type is the most significant to autumn bird hunters, without all four habitats in proximity, woodcock won't be abundant.

In spring, woodcock go through an elaborate mating ritual. A male flies in straight upward circles, then spirals back down while singing a "chisharee chisharee" song to attract a mate. This happens on a "singing ground." After mating, the hen lays four eggs in a shallow, leaf-lined depression, then raises the young in lowland thickets.

Come fall, woodcock are migratory—an imperative dictated by their dietary staple of worms. They aren't into bill-bending on frozen soil, so they follow food availability south. During years of normal temperatures and precipitation, migration is more a sustained trickle-through of individuals than here-today-gone-tomorrow inundations. Birds start to shift southward in leisurely move-ments often by late September, though over much of their breeding range migra-tion numbers peak about the third week of October. In the North, woodcock drop off after the first week of November, per-haps sooner depending on weather.

Although uncommon, large flights can occur, again usually triggered by weather. I've experienced several of these mass arrivals—a cover that's bar-ren one morning can have woodcock ping-ponging everywhere the next. Consider yourself fortunate if the gods of Yankee weather grant you these siz-able flights of woodcock.

Woodcock range.

Woodcock are worth pursuing for the sake of woodcock ... not as just an afterthought to the fabled ruffed grouse.

by more superficially spectacular birds, the wood-cock is a sought-after upland species. Biologists estimate that hunters annually invest 3 to 4 mil-lion days in pursuit of woodcock and when pushed admit that the number is likely higher. These days, woodcock are upstaging competitors.

Look at it this way. Despite a population slump due mainly to habitat loss, woodcock are usually plentiful in suitable cover. Although the massive migratory flights of hunter mythology just ain't so, top coverts can draw sizable numbers of birds. Rest assured; woodcock will be in woodcock cover, if not today, then tomorrow (see sidebar "Finding Woodcock" on page 57).

HUNTING TIPS & TACTICS

Serious woodcock hunters usually maintain a collection of U.S. Geological Survey topographic maps for locating covers. These maps show roads,

53

rivers and their drainages (even old homesteads) and are configured with contours indicating slopes and bottomlands. Maps provide an accurate look at landforms and allow you to pinpoint potential habitat without aimlessly banging around in the woods.

Seek out cover such as diverse hardwood stands spreading out from river valleys and feeder creeks. Once in that cover, look for telltale signs such as bore holes from worm-probing bills. Worms are at least 80 percent water, which forces woodcock to eat their weight of them in a 24-hour period.

What goes in must come out, and a daily wad of worms whips through the birds and splashes the forest floor with obvious chalky, brown-streaked blobs the size of a half-dollar. Fore and aft—especially aft—woodcock advertise their presence.

Flushing Birds

When you find woodcock honey-holes, hunt them carefully and methodically. Don't be in a hurry.

If you use a dog—and most hunters do—let him handle the hard work of weaving through thickets and shouldering into the density of alders. But he must hunt close; 50 yards is a fair working range for a pointer, while a flusher should hunt at 10 to 15 yards. Because you won't always be able to see your dog, he should wear a bell or an electronic beeper, otherwise you won't have a clue where he is or what he is doing. Occasionally woodcock hold within feet of a pointer's nose. The temptation is to look for the bird, but unless you want to see it more than shoot it, just walk in for the flush. Don't waste time scanning the ground at the expense of positioning yourself for a shot.

Lacking a dog, you'll have to beat the bushes on your own. Use a walk-and-stop tactic to weave through small pieces of habitat like creekbottoms, tight corners where vegetation changes and pasture edges where fields give way to young trees. And stay alert because you'll have no warning. There will be a twittering flush and the bird will be gone. Always accurately mark a downed bird. Dead or alive, woodcock are beautifully camouflaged and unlike a dog, you can't smell them.

Either way, dog or not, woodcock cover is full of whippy, thorny "stuff" that slaps and digs hunter flesh. If you value your eyes, wear shooting glasses. Wear light gloves to keep your hands from looking like you lost a fight with barbed wire.

Woodcock Wisdom

The logical end of a woodcock flush should be to a hunter tumbling the bird in a puff of feathers.

It looks so simple. Even a subpar wing shot ought to dust woodcock fluttering skyward like big moths.

Sometimes it happens that way. Often it doesn't.

Why? For one thing, woodcock are small targets about the size of a fist; for another, they aren't the pokey flyers they appear to be. They need only a moment to accelerate from a sudden and erratic vertical flush; then they evaporate into screening foliage. Add side-slipping through dense cover to uncanny skill at swapping directions, and you have deceptive fistfuls of feathers that leave off-balance gunners wondering what happened.

Don't get in a rush when you're hunting woodcock. Move through cover slowly and methodically. If you have a dog, make sure he works close—50 yards for a pointer, 10 to 15 for a flusher.

Shotguns & Loads for Woodcock

An old homespun cliché says hunters never ruin shotguns by cutting off a couple inches of barrel to get rid of length, weight and choke. Nowhere is that advice closer to the mark than in a woodcock gun.

Shoot any type of shotgun that works for you, but leave the heavy artillery at home. Woodcock require finesse, not firepower, which translates into streamlined and maneuverable guns. These days, many woodcock hunters favor lighter double guns with side-by-side or stacked barrels about 26 inches long. Doubles handle smoothly and eliminate excess inches of receiver found in pumps and autoloaders. Besides, woodcock hunters rarely need more than two shots at a time.

If ever a game bird and shotgun gauge were perfectly matched, they are the woodcock and the 20, with the 28 gauge holding a modest second. No woodcock hunter needs anything more potent than a 20; nonetheless, the 12 gauge is widely used. One reason is the 12's ballistic efficiency when loaded light for birds like woodcock.

Another is ammunition availability. Any country store carries a range of 12 gauge ammo, while 20 gauge shells can be in short supply. And 28s? Bring your own box.

Woodcock are small and thin-skinned; fairly hit, they fall easily. As a case in point, market hunters preferred tiny shot size—No. 10s or 12s—and they were shooting for cash. The best pure woodcock load today is No. 9 shot in skeet ammo. However, because ruffed grouse are often found alongside woodcock, most hunters compromise with No. 8s in low-based target loads.

Woodcock shooting takes place at close range and is best done with open bores. For early-season hunting when leaves are dense, good choke choices are cylinder or skeet. As the covers open and shots lengthen a bit, switch to improved cylinder.

In a nutshell, an all-around combination that will anchor woodcock under any conditions is a fast-swinging 12 or 20 gauge sporting a 26-inch barrel choked improved cylinder and loaded with No. 8s.

A fine fistful of feathers indeed. Twenty and 28 gauges are perfect for woodcock, though a 12 will do the job. When combined with cylinder, skeet or improved-cylinder chokes, low-brass No. 8 or No. 9 shotshells are perfect.

Woodcock cover is tight, and shots are close. If you can, try to take birds at the peak of their corkscrew flush, before they level off to fly away. Rest assured, woodcock are never very easy to hit.

Hunter legend holds that woodcock tower rapidly, then change gears and level off just above the cover; the time to shoot is when they peak. And it works—but only if the birds cooperate. Just as often, they'll flush low or corkscrew up and zig when you expect them to zag, or twist in mid-flush to fly straight at you. In other words, be ready for anything.

Woodcock hunting is a tight-cover, close-quarters sport in which most gunplay is under 25 yards; during the early season it is often at 15 yards. Mostly, you get the birds close or you don't get them at all. But if the cover is right, there are times when it pays to wait a second or two before touching off a shot. To give themselves an edge, savvy hunters tote guns that are light and maneuverable, with open chokes and loaded with target ammo.

WOODCOCK & GUN DOGS

A case can be made for hunting other birds without a dog, but it's far less justifiable with woodcock. A dogless hunter will walk past many more birds than he'll flush, and if he does knock one down, lacking a dog he has no more than an even chance of finding it. Practicality aside, a hunter alone loses the elegance of dogs hunting birds uniquely matched to them. Indeed, knowledgeable hunters consider woodcock to be

heaven-sent for dogs. With their heavy odor and willingness to stand crowding, they are easy birds for average dogs to work, yet they have enough quirks to challenge good dogs.

Woodcock can be hunted with any breed or working style of gun dog. I've shot more woodcock over "flush 'n fetchers"—spaniels and retrievers—than over pointing dogs. But that is a matter of choice; I like the fast action of well-honed flushers.

That said, there is no doubt that the classic woodcock dogs are English setters and pointers, though breeds like the Brittany and German shorthair are edging up in popularity. Even hard-core flushing dog fanciers will admit that a lot of woodcock can be taken with decent pointing dogs. Whatever the breed, the keys to a woodcock dog are controlled birdwork and willingness to retrieve.

Having a good, close-working dog, whether a pointer or a flusher, makes woodcock hunting even more joyful.

The morning air has warmed, and my springer is up on his toes. He knows that woodcock are close, likely hunkered down in brambles surrounding nearby arthritic-limbed apple trees. The waiting is over.

Beneath the trees, the earth is white-dappled with woodcock splashes. A bird jumps wild, away from the spaniel who does not hear the soft flush. I watch the woodcock wing away, then refocus on my dog making game at the brambles' edge. He drops his head and homes in to drive the bird skyward. He sits at the flush and marks the towering flight, waiting for the shot and the command to retrieve. He hears both and arrows to the bird. Then he is in front of me, bright-eyed and bearing a long-billed treasure.

It is autumn—the season of woodcock—and birds are in the covers.

Finding Woodcock

Most woodcock spend spring breeding seasons and summers in the North and remain there until the chill winds of autumn goose them south to warmer climes. This is why fine early and mid-fall woodcock hunting is found from Nova Scotia across southern Ontario, and from Maine along the northern tier of states—especially New York, Pennsylvania, Michigan and Wisconsin on into Minnesota.

If you hit it right and the flight is in—or you keep hunting until it comes through your neck of the woods—the hunting can be grand on a fine fall day.

Come cold weather, woodcock migrate to wintering grounds along the southern Atlantic and Gulf Coasts, with Louisiana tallying the largest concentrations of birds. Depending on the birds' origins and the capricious nature of winter, these fugitives may escape cold weather from the Carolinas to Florida, Arkansas to East Texas.

If I were to plan a custom woodcock hunting trip—assuming typical weather conditions—early October would find me in southern New Brunswick. From there I would drop into eastern Maine and hunt regrowing clear-cuts. A week later, I'd be in Michigan where I would stay until the birds thinned. During mid-November, I would head to covers in the vicinity of the Mississippi River in southwestern Tennessee or eastern Arkansas. Where I would be in mid-December to mid-January is no surprise. You'd find me haunting the southeastern parishes of Louisiana, wearing rubber boots and following tight-hunting dogs in the hardwood bottoms along the drainages of rivers like the Mississippi and Atchafalaya.

Chapter 5

BLUE GROUSE: A ROCKY MOUNTAIN ADVENTURE

BY CHRIS MADSON

Blue grouse will take you far and high into the great Rockies, to the land of pine, spruce, fir and aspen (far left). The bird is named for the male's dusky blue-gray plumage (left), although the description "mountain grouse" would be just as apt.

I'd like to say it was intuition, the kind of feel for cover and birds that comes from years of boondocking. Actually, it was blind luck.

After 15 minutes of grinding up the two-track in low-range four-wheel drive, the front of the truck dropped and we came out on a tiny plateau that seemed almost horizontal as long as I didn't think about it too hard.

"This looks good," Cody said as he set the emergency brake.

I considered the mountainside, an open stand of lodgepole pine with an occasional clump of aspen in the drainages below. The timber

stretched out of sight in front of us.

"What makes you say so?"

"First place I've seen where we could park. Listen, would you put a rock behind that wheel?"

We chocked the truck, uncased the guns, and headed south along the contour. A few hundred yards along the slope, I stepped into the head of a draw, dry at this time of year but with enough moisture to support a thick stand of arnica. I waded into the cover and headed downhill, scrambling over hidden deadfalls with my gun over my head.

I was teetering on a pile of downed timber

when the blue exploded. It was a classic ruffed grouse chance—the bird clipped through a couple of branches and was just disappearing into a screen of aspen when the pattern got there. A shower of leaves and twigs spattered down out of the canopy.

"Get him?" Cody was 40 yards to the left and completely invisible.

"Not sure."

I walked over to my mark and peered down through the vegetation. A feather, and another. And the bird. An adult hen.

"We might want to check across from here," I said. We swung up out of the drainage onto the grass under the pines. Cody went left around a rock pile the size of a Victorian mansion while I made my way up a crack to the right. Up above, there was a shady patch of grass with a ponderosa pine uprooted in the middle. As Cody walked into the clearing, I saw three blues step around the root wad.

"Hold up," I told him. "I've got birds over here. I'll flush them to you."

Cody set his feet and I rushed the birds. Two ducked back around the roots while the third jumped to the right over the log. I snap-shot just as he cleared the bole. As the bird tumbled out of sight, Cody shot on the other side of the clearing.

"Did those other two fly?" I inquired as I retrieved my bird.

"They'd have walked right over the ridge if I'd let 'em. The second one took off after I sluiced the first one."

"Sluiced?"

"That's the way we do it in Wyoming. There was no way they were gonna fly. And mama really does like her blue grouse."

I shook my head in mock disbelief.

"And what was that shot you took?" he went on.

"He was in the air."

"He was hopping up on that log."

And so it went as we headed into the next drainage, Cody explaining the difference between a hop and a flush while I extolled the lightning-quick reflexes it takes to catch an unwilling blue in his upward trajectory.

High-country parks offering a mix of cover—meadows, brush, young aspen and mature conifers—make perfect blue grouse country. You'll walk and walk and walk and walk … and then find all the birds at once.

BIRD OF THE WILDERNESS, BIRD OF MIGRATION

My tale describes the good news—and the bad news—about blue grouse hunting.

On the down side, the blue grouse is the ultimate "fool's hen." This isn't a result of some flaw in the bird's innate survival skills, as much as a reflection of its habitat. Blue grouse live in the mixed forests along the spine of the continent from Alaska and the Yukon to New Mexico and Arizona. They routinely cope with all of America's most dangerous predators—weasels to wolves, goshawks to grizzlies. But one predator is missing. In many parts of blue grouse country, generations of the birds can live and die without ever meeting a human being!

As a result, most blue grouse you'll meet simply don't recognize a human as a threat. The birds will walk away from you as you approach, and if you rush them, they'll fly just far enough to feel safe, often landing a few feet out of reach in a nearby tree. Throw sticks at them, and they will likely duck or hop around to the far side of the trunk. This can be frustrating for a scattergunner who's spent the entire summer honing his wing-shooting skills and wants to show off.

And that isn't the end of the frustration.

The blue grouse is a moving target in a different sense than most upland birds. A bobwhite might live out his life within a quarter mile of where he was hatched; even a pheasant is unlikely to range more than a mile or two in the course of a year. Most blue grouse routinely migrate several miles between summer and winter quarters, and this migration is generally straight up.

PLENTY OF REASONS TO HUNT BLUES

So why even bother with blue grouse? I think there are several reasons.

Possibly most important is the country blue grouse frequent. They inhabit the wildest part of North America—the big ridges of the Rockies, Sierras, and Coast Range—from the edge between grass, shrub and timber below almost to treeline above.

Truth be told, a blue grouse is beautiful on a dinner plate too, with meat as light-colored and mild as that of any ruffed grouse. Plus, he weighs about three pounds when he thumps the ground after your shot; that's a good-sized grouse indeed.

Much of this land is held in public trust, open to any hunter with enough grit to walk it. And, over most of the bird's range, there's practically no competition—most of the people who hunt this ground are looking for elk or mule deer, not feathers.

Then there is the bird. The blue is North America's second largest grouse—an adult male might weigh three pounds. Females and young wear the barred brown camouflage typical of the hens and chicks of most game birds, but males are charcoal to slate gray with red combs over their eyes, a tasteful but striking combination that makes a fine trophy. And, unlike the prairie grouse, the blue is a light-meat bird; nothing is better on the table.

This last quality is why many elk hunters carry .22 pistols in the timber—it's legal to shoot blue grouse on the ground in many Western states, and a blue grouse feed is one of the great triumphs of camp cuisine. Potting a grouse with a handgun may seem unsporting, but don't knock it until you've tried it. It calls for some moderately fancy marksmanship, especially if you insist on holding for the head.

Understanding Blue Grouse

Blue grouse are tough birds.

They're one of a handful of creatures that spend the winter in the high Rockies. They don't hibernate, and they actually fatten up as the winter progresses. The secret of their success is their diet—they might be the only species besides the moose that can digest conifer needles. When conditions are particularly rugged, blue grouse might roost in the snow, but they spend most of the winter in the branches of dense conifer forests just below timberline.

A male blue grouse displays his springtime bachelorhood. Hoots accompany the show, as an additional advertisement to hens.

When the snow begins to dwindle and the days lengthen, most of the adults move down off the ridges to the lower edge of the forest. Males establish territories and defend them with a peculiar hooting call and a display called the flutter flight. In the dense timber along the coast, blue grouse hoot louder to make themselves heard; in the thinner timber of the Rocky Mountain interior, the hooting is softer. Males usually prefer to display on their own, but there are occasional reports of several males and females gathering for a communal courtship like prairie grouse. After breeding, the males return to the high timber while most hens venture out into the grass and shrubs to nest.

Broods are fairly small for a chicken-like bird, generally around four chicks per hen. These family groups feed in grasslands for a month or more after hatching, focusing on a diet of insects that provides the protein that the chicks need for growth and that the hen needs to grow new feathers after molt.

In early August, the broods start uphill toward wintering areas. Taking greens, berries and seeds as long as they are available, blues focus more and more on conifer needles as the year progresses. Where Douglas fir is available, blue grouse seem to prefer it, but they will eat a variety of pine needles, larch, fir and juniper as well. They have a talent for finding trees with the most digestible needles.

Blue grouse range.

A good bird dog will find more blues than you can on your own. And he'll get them airborne for you too.

HUNTING STRATEGIES & TACTICS

If your notion of sport absolutely demands an explosive flush and a half-mile escape flight, blue grouse are bound to disappoint you. But there are ways you can encourage the birds to do what you want them to do.

First, use a dog. The average blue grouse might never have met a human being. But the bird has met a host of four-footed hunters, and he gives them all the respect they deserve. A disciplined bird dog will find more blues than you can find yourself, and he's more likely to convince the birds to fly in the bargain. Most blue grouse are well mannered in front of a good pointing dog; they hold as well as the typical bobwhite, maybe even better. If your dog likes to range, consider using a bell or beeper collar—most of this cover is thick.

And, if you find a productive grouse covert, make sure you remember it. Assuming that you leave a few birds for seed, you can educate the local blues in the fine art of hunter evasion and may end up with more sport than you can handle.

Finding Blues

Bear in mind that when you find grouse is often as important as where, especially at lower elevations. Hens and broods are moving toward treeline throughout the fall; they'll be much higher on the mountain in October than they were in early September.

Shotguns & Loads for Blues

In the Rocky Mountain states, most blue grouse are probably taken with .30-06, .270 and .300 Win. Mag. using sturdy bullets between 130 and 200 grains. These choices of armament don't reflect the ferocity of the blue grouse as a game animal; they arise from the tendency of most Westerners to take blue grouse in mixed bags with bull elk.

When it comes to wing shooting, blue grouse are a slightly larger version of ruffed grouse. They live in thick cover and hold well, presenting close shots at every possible angle. Once they decide to get airborne, they can be as hard to nail as ruffed grouse, but they aren't hard to knock down, and once they hit the ground, they generally don't run far.

So if you're coming west after blues, bring your favorite ruffed grouse gun and load. I lean toward a 20 gauge over-and-under choked "skeet" or "improved cylinder." Seven-eighths of an ounce of 7½ shot is a more-than-adequate load.

Though they're bigger birds, blue grouse will tumble just fine to the same guns, chokes and loads you might use for ruffs.

Blue grouse hunting will definitely reduce the thickness of your boot soles. A good rule of thumb is to start high. Then be methodical as you search. Blue grouse are notorious for being one place one week, then somewhere totally different the next.

It can be hard to recognize a spot that offers better blue grouse forage and cover than another. Blues have broad tastes in cuisine. During late summer, they continue to eat the protein-rich insects that support growth of young and replacement of feathers after molt in adults. Blues also dote on seeds, greens and berries and, as the growing season wanes, they turn more and more regularly to a blue grouse staple—conifer needles.

They seem to prefer Douglas fir when they can find it, but various pines, larch and junipers are just about as good. Some trees are more nutritious than others, and blues are masters at finding the best. Since they typically nip off two-thirds of the needle and leave the base, a heavily browsed tree takes on a hedged look by the end of the winter—a good sign that there are grouse around.

Walking the Walk

Millions of acres of the West's high timber seem to offer adequate blue grouse habitat, but the birds know what they want. A detailed log of past hunts is a valuable tool for any serious blue grouse hunter. A precise map of productive coverts is even better.

It should come as no surprise that successful blue grouse hunters are not generally inclined to share the locations of their secret spots with strangers. This leaves most of us to prospect on our own, a daunting proposition in the high country. If you're not in shape when you start the blue grouse season, you will be at the end. And you might save some wear on your Vibram if you keep a couple guidelines in mind:

First, start at the top. Blue grouse do much of their courting at the lower edge of high-country timber where the trees meet shrubs and grass. Once the breeding is over, adult males adjourn to the top of the mountain, typically hanging out within a few hundred feet of treeline. By mid-summer, they have been joined by hens who have lost their broods. Hens with broods spend much of the summer on the lower edge of the timber, but by early August, they have started the upward migration toward the zone of limber pine, white-bark pine, Engleman spruce and subalpine fir where they will spend the winter.

By the time hunting seasons open in most states, hens and their broods will be scattered up and down the mountainside, while adult males and barren hens will be on the high edge of the timber. As the season continues, these adults will be joined by the grouse families coming up the hill. From a hunter's point of view, the easiest place to start looking for grouse is on a national forest with roads at timberline. Timber edges are good places to start hunting—if it has been a good berry year, stands of whortleberry, huckleberry or snowberry near the woods often hold blues.

Second, be methodical. While many people are convinced that the typical blue grouse is dumber than a sack of pea gravel, the don't-draw-attention-to-yourself strategy is actually pretty effective. It's easy for a hunter—human or otherwise—to walk past a shadow-colored bird sitting quietly in the shade of an aspen grove or a tangle of pine or fir. The bird probably won't fly or run to give himself away, so you or your dog will have to get close to find him.

If you are in one of those mixed coverts of older roost trees and grass, shrubbery and forbs, don't just stroll through it. Get down near the bottom of the good stuff and walk the contour, then move up 50 yards and work back. Three or four passes should stir the birds if any are around.

You have to love blue grouse if for nothing else than the high-country coverts they pull you to. Blues are truly citizens of the wilderness.

If you have a dog, you can afford to make wider sweeps.

MILES & ADVENTURE

Finally, a little scouting won't hurt your blue grouse hunting success. Cruise the forest service roads near timberline, and you'll eventually stumble across some blues. Take a good look at the cover they're using and keep it in mind for later. And don't do all your scouting in the pickup. There are worse ways to spend a late-August Saturday than strolling the high ridges. You could find some birds, and you'll surely find some likely coverts.

Probably more important, you'll put the springs back in your legs and the wind back in your lungs. If you intend to do much blue grouse hunting, those are two commodities you will definitely need. ✦

Finding Blue Grouse

Blue grouse are listed as legal game in New Mexico, Arizona, California, Nevada, Utah, Colorado, Wyoming, Idaho, Oregon, Washington, Montana, Alberta, British Columbia, Yukon, Northwest Territories and Alaska. Seasons typically open in early September; Alaska seasons open in early to mid-August.

One of the great benefits of being a blue grouse hunter is the availability of hunting land. Most good blue grouse habitat is publicly owned—frequently, national forest land.

Not all blue grouse are taken with a fancy scattergun shot over an elegant dog. Sometimes the hunting is just huntin' ... and that's fine.

Chapter 6

SPRUCE GROUSE: TREKKING TO THE WILDEST PLACES

BY WAYNE VAN ZWOLL

*T*hough its range spans a good chunk of North America, little has been written about the spruce grouse. That's mainly because this bird lives in the wildest of wild places and is reclusive by nature.

Spruce grouse inhabit conifer forests almost exclusively, feeding on pine and spruce needles most of the year. From the Alaska Peninsula to the Maine Coast, from central Idaho to north-eastern Labrador, spruce grouse are pretty much the same compact bird: a bit stockier than a ruffed grouse but not as big as a blue grouse. Females look about the same in all parts of their range. Males of *Dendragapus canadensis canadensis*, the Northeastern subspecies, differ in appearance and behavior from males of *D. c. franklinii*, the Franklin, or Southwestern subspecies.

Known as the "fool hen" in parts of its range for its trusting demeanor, the spruce grouse gets relatively little hunting pressure. In parts of its range, it is protected.

Whether you're in alpine mountains or vast Northern forests, dark-colored spruce grouse (cock, far left) will never be far from their namesake tree. That said, finding the birds (hen, near left) is never easy to do. You have to do a lot of walking in some very lonely places.

Still, the spruce grouse is a handsome bird, and good eating. Continent-wide, its population is stable, though habitat change (mainly fire and logging) causes local fluctuations, some dramatic.

FIND THE HABITAT

Once you find spruce grouse, the hunting can be great, and relatively easy. Finding good grouse habitat is the trick—the part of the hunt that will wear off some boot leather. Here's how to save some steps!

67

Spruce grouse live near conifers, but not always in spruce forests. In fact, over much of its range, the bird prefers pine timber. Young stands of jack-pine and lodgepole pine are good places to look for grouse in the Rockies. Alaskan birds are more often found in spruce lowlands. The black spruce woodlands in Minnesota hold lots of birds, as do thickets of red fir and balsam fir in Maine. The mountains of the Pacific Northwest provide grouse cover in high-altitude stands of subalpine fir. On the West Coast, these birds inhabit hemlock forests.

Dense stands of trees 12 to 40 feet high, with well-developed middle stories, are prime habitat for spruce grouse. A thick shrub layer also attracts grouse. Snow moves the birds to places with heavy canopy; fair weather and melting snow in the canopy puts the grouse into more open habitat.

In the fall, the birds are occasionally found in stands of alder, willow and other riparian (streamside) trees. By mid-November, regardless of snow conditions, they are almost always up in the conifers, and that's where they stay most of the winter.

Spruce, pine and lodgepole forests will all hold birds. In the early fall, alders, willows and other hardwoods will harbor birds too, if there is grouse food of interest there—especially berries. Hunt all openings and edges!

KNOW WHAT THEY EAT

Understanding the spruce grouse's foraging habits can also help you find birds.

Pine needles are the primary forage in winter, whether or not snow is on the ground. Hunters should know that larch needles figure heavily in autumn diets. The growing tips and flowers and fruits of blueberry bushes are also high in carbohydrates. Grouse eat them readily, and love berries of all kinds, particularly blueberries and cranberries, anytime.

The low quality and digestibility of conifer needles has prompted questions as to how spruce grouse can survive in winter on a diet containing almost nothing else. The answer: Low energy demands and vast quantities of needles combine to see the grouse through. In spring, breeding females need other, higher quality food to nest successfully.

HUNTING TECHNIQUES & TIPS

Spruce grouse are walkers, rarely taking to wing and then flying only a short distance to perch in a tree to escape danger on the ground. They appear overly trusting and may sit on a branch even when approached. Sometimes a grouse on the ground will not even fly but will simply walk away from a hunter. These traits can make the wing shooting dificult in a way few hunters expect!

Hunting is best in the early season. Late in hunting seasons, spruce grouse may seem to disappear. Apparently influenced more by day length than by snowfall, the birds begin to live almost totally in trees. Birds visible on the ground in summer and autumn are then hidden in the mid-crowns of conifers.

Escape flight can take two

Understanding the Spruce Grouse

About the size of willow ptarmigan, which share parts of its range, spruce grouse differ in that their plumage does not turn white in winter. Unlike the blue grouse, which occurs with Franklin grouse in the northern Rockies, spruce grouse males have no inflatable vocal sac.

Males and females are both dark-colored birds; white-barred black bellies distiguish the hens from ruffed grouse hens. Also, there's a pale band on the end of a spruce grouse's tail. Males are distinctively barred on the back; in breeding season they erect scarlet patches above their eyes.

Spruce grouse males drum to attract hens, but not as loudly as ruffed grouse. Stamping, barely audible, is done to chase other males off breeding grounds. Egg laying commences in late May and early June. The nest is a shallow depression in the ground, lined with grasses, twigs and short tail feathers from the hen.

During the summer the hen stays close to her brood, and the family moves as a unit in search of food. Foraging in open areas is a trade-off: The chicks are more visible and vulnerable to predators, but there's also more food—insects and young plants—where the sun warms the ground. Most losses to predators come before and just after the hatch. Red squirrels are the most serious threat to grouse eggs. Coyotes, foxes, bobcats, lynx, weasels and forest hawks and owls take the young birds. Predation is, in fact, the biggest single cause of mortality in spruce grouse and can account for the loss of more birds than all other causes combined.

While predators have the greatest effect on individual survival, trends in grouse populations are heavily influenced by habitat change. Fire and logging can create better habitat for grouse, which require young, actively growing trees and thick vegetation at mid-canopy. But disturbance that results in complete deforestation can remove spruce grouse from an area.

A male spruce grouse displays his dark-feathered finery, and bright red eye comb, to attract females for mating. He drums too, though not as loudly as a ruff does.

Spruce grouse range.

forms. Most commonly, the grouse lifts quietly (compared to ruffed and blue grouse) off the ground and flies with surprising grace through the trees. Rarely does it fly far or go very high. The other flight mode is in response to an attack by hawk or owl, in which case the grouse climbs noisily above the treetops, then levels off in a long, fast cruise to clear the area. But spruce grouse are not adapted for sustained flight, so survival depends primarily on reaching cover quickly, and they are as likely to walk there as fly there.

You don't need a dog to hunt spruce grouse, though one will expand your range and presumably increase the number of birds you see. A dog also helps you find downed birds, though in typical spruce grouse habitat this is not nearly so difficult as in the tangles of brush favored by ruffed grouse.

You'll walk a lot hunting spruce grouse, so wearing good boots, packing a hearty lunch and carrying plenty of water make sense. Remember that late in the season, even if heavy snows haven't hit, the grouse will be in the trees, and you might walk under birds that never show themselves. The best spruce grouse hunting is in early- and mid-season, when ground-story brush has lost some of its foliage but before seasonal flights into the conifers.

The spruce grouse's tendency to sit tight rather than flush is why the bird is sometimes called "fool hen." But this habit is a function of the remoteness of the bird's habitat, rather than an indication of its intelligence. Spruce grouse have survived predation for untold ages by calmly walking away or sitting tight, rather than flying away in a panic. Don't blame the bird!

So you might have to work to get a bird to fly if you want your spruce grouse dinner to tumble out of the air. But if you're in an area that gets some hunting pressure, don't be surprised if the birds get cagey—and flush wild—like ruffed grouse would.

Roadways and streambed corridors make great places to hunt spruce grouse. The birds like to peck for the grit and gravel, and the openings provide shooting lanes in an otherwise densely treed landscape. Streamsides are also good places to hunt because birds are drawn there for the berries and other attractive foods (such as mush-

Shotguns & Loads for Spruce Grouse

You can kill spruce grouse handily with 20-bore shotguns and modest loads of 7½ shot. But I prefer a 12 gauge with 1¼ ounces of No. 6 shot and a 3¼-dram-equivalent charge of powder. Shots are typically close because spruce grouse let you get close. On the other hand, if you find them in the trees, or if the forest is particularly thick, you might have to chop some brush with your shot before it gets to the target. Also, a grouse barreling out of a tree accelerates quicker than one jumping from behind a log, putting more distance behind it while you shoulder your gun.

A lightweight shotgun, such as Browning's Citori Lightning, helps you point fast and keeps you fresh as you hike. I favor improved-cylinder and modified chokes in short barrels. Another good choice is the Benelli Montefeltro, a lightweight autoloader.

Don't undergun yourself for spruce grouse. Your shot might have to whack through dense brush before it reaches the bird.

rooms and forbs) that grow where sunlight reaches the ground.

If you venture into the dense forest, check out openings. Like other forest grouse species, sprucies prefer edge habitat where sunlight and shade together increase the variety of plant life.

A RARE BIRD IN THE BAG

Many upland hunters travel far to chase the variety of great game birds that call North America home. The spruce grouse may well be the most elusive species of all, if for nothing else than the remote, forested habitat it lives in. You will work hard to get to spruce grouse country, and then walk long to find birds within its vastness.

If you're a serious bird hunter, you owe yourself a go at spruce grouse in the wildest of wild places where this fascinating bird lives.

Spruce grouse draw hunters to some wild and beautiful places they otherwise wouldn't visit. That alone is enough reason to pursue these rare and unique game birds.

Finding Spruce Grouse

Getting to a place with an open spruce grouse hunting season may be more difficult than actually shooting a bird once you get there.

Maine has much of the spruce grouse range in the northeastern U.S., but the birds are protected there. In fact, Maine hunting regulations carry illustrations showing the differences between spruce grouse and ruffed grouse to minimize accidental shootings.

Currently, spruce grouse are legal game in Minnesota, where the limit is five birds daily. Hunters enjoy a season that runs from mid-September to the end of the year. No hunting is permitted in Michigan or Wisconsin though.

On the western end of the continent, Franklin grouse may be shot in Washington and Idaho, where most of the U.S. birds are found. Seasons open the first of September and close December 31. You can try for a daily bag of four birds in Idaho along the Salmon and Payette Rivers and in the northern Panhandle. Washington's three-bird limit is easiest to earn in the northern Cascade Range.

In Canada, populations of spruce grouse remain generally sound, with particularly high numbers in northern Alberta and in Ontario around Virginiatown. September through December seasons apply. In Ontario, spruce grouse are commonly called partridge, a confusing name that also describes ruffed grouse in the upper Midwest and northeastern U.S.

Alaska has generally good populations of spruce grouse on the upper Kuskokwim, Yukon and Tanana Rivers. The Kenai Peninsula also offers good hunting. Statewide, the birds may be now on a slow slide, apparently due to deterioration of white spruce stands.

Chapter 7

PTARMIGAN: GUNNING THE TUNDRA

BY JUDD COONEY

"Yessir, soon's I get my caribou I want to hunt some of them peter migeons," drawled the Georgia bowhunter as outfitter Dave Neel and I climbed out of Dave's 4x4 pickup at caribou camp on the north slope of Alaska's Brooks Range.

"You want to hunt what?" Dave asked, totally befuddled by the request.

Whether you're on the tundra of the far, far north (far left) or climbing rocky alpine mountaintops (left), ptarmigan hunting is tough work. But the shooting is fun ... when you finally find the birds.

"You know, them little brown and white grouse-like birds that keep bustin' out of the willows every time I stalk a caribou," reiterated the serious bowhunter. "You mean ptarmigan," laughed Dave as he finally figured out what his client was talking about.

Ptarmigan (tar-mi-gen) are probably the most underhunted and least-known upland game bird in North America. I can remember a few years back when I took a couple of friends ptarmigan hunting above timberline along the Continental Divide south of Corona Pass and west of Denver. Neither had hunted or seen a ptarmigan before. On the jolting jeep drive to the high alpine ridges, I tried to convince my skeptical companions that the variegated feathering on these little grouse made them almost invisible on the boulder- and scree-covered slopes they called home. And their preference for remaining motionless rather than running or flying made them extremely hard to spot.

After an hour of ankle-twisting and blister-raising sidehilling on the steep, rocky slopes without seeing a bird, my compadres started chiding me with, "Here's a big fat one," as they picked up a hefty rock or, "Hey, there's a whole flock of them," as they pointed to a scree slope covered with boulders.

Understanding Ptarmigan

Ptarmigan are close relatives of the forest and prairie grouse. But ptarmigan have adapted to alpine and arctic tundra throughout the Northern Hemisphere.

Ptarmigan weigh from 10 oz. to 1½ pounds and are the only game bird to turn white in winter. This white plumage is an excellent insulator against the frigid cold, because the colorless feather filaments are filled with insulating dead air rather than color pigment. A ptarmigan's fully feathered feet act like snowshoes, keeping him afloat and mobile on soft snow. Ptarmigan actually roost "under" the snow for warmth, and as protection from winged and four-legged predators. They will dive-bomb into a snowbank to bury themselves completely. Ptarmigan can actually gain weight during the harsh winters because many protein-rich buds and berries become more accessible atop the deep and

White-tailed ptarmigan inhabit high-altitude, alpine tundra—rocky meadows and ridgetops on top of the world.

drifting snow.

Ptarmigan are renowned for their boom-and-bust population fluctuations. Some years there are more ptarmigan in an area than you can fire a shotgun at. A year later you can run the pads off a good dog and not find a single bird anywhere. The swing between overabundance and a total lack of birds within a short period of time remains a mystery to bird biologists. It could be tied to harsh winter conditions, bad hatching or chick-rearing conditions or any number of other factors unique to this species and their often hostile environment.

The **white-tailed ptarmigan**, *Lagopus leucurus*, is the smallest of the three kinds of ptarmigan and is the only ptarmigan limited to North America and found in the lower 48 states. Its range extends from Alaska along the Rocky Mountains to the northern border of New Mexico. White-tailed ptarmigan, as the name indicates, are the only ptarmigan without black feathers in the tail. Whitetails are high-altitude dwellers and are found on the alpine meadows and rocky ridgetops.

Willow ptarmigan, *Lagopus lagopus*, are the largest members of the ptarmigan family, as well as the most widely spread and numerous of the three kinds of ptarmigan. This tundra dweller occupies a broad range throughout Alaska, where it is the state bird, and Canada's north country. Willow ptarmigan are also common in Scandinavia and Russia. The male willow ptarmigan has more reddish color than either of its cousins and a proportionately larger bill. The female willow ptarmigan and the rock ptarmigan are almost indistinguishable.

Rock ptarmigan, *Lagopus mutus*, are very similar in appearance to the willow ptarmigan but a bit smaller. Rock ptarmigan inhabit most of Alaska and northern Canada except for the westernmost flat tundra and coastal areas. Rock ptarmigan are also common throughout Greenland, Iceland, Scandinavia and Eurasia. Isolated populations can

Willow ptarmigan inhabit alpine tundra of the northland—Canada and Alaska.

also be found in northern Japan, Switzerland and Spain. These ptarmigan prefer the large treeless mountain and foothill areas at mid elevations. In some areas of Alaska and Canada, you can bag both rock and willow ptarmigan in the same day.

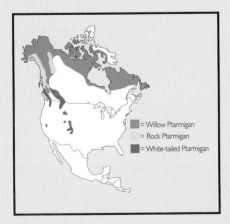

= Willow Ptarmigan
= Rock Ptarmigan
= White-tailed Ptarmigan

Ptarmigan range.

Finally, I spotted a subtle movement in the rocks at the lower edge of a receding snowbank and nonchalantly asked my companions if they wanted to break for a cold drink. They agreed wholeheartedly and while they were grumbling about the lack of birds and unloading their packs to get out sodas and a candy bar, I knelt down and filled my three-bird ptarmigan limit with three shots from my Colt .22 Match Target pistol. A flock of about twenty birds had been virtually invisible in the rocks 30 yards from us, completely unnoticed by my hunting partners.

Ptarmigan are fun to hunt—even with a shotgun!—and quite often they can be pursued in conjunction with big game hunting junkets. I've taken ptarmigan while caribou and moose hunting on the Alaskan and Canadian tundra, and high in the Colorado Rockies on mule deer, elk and sheep hunting trips.

There have been times when I've been big game hunting in ptarmigan country where the noisy little grouse have been everywhere, cackling and carrying on, making it difficult for me to keep my focus on my intended quarry. Then when I did take time to pursue the birds in earnest, I couldn't find a blooming one. This is typical of ptarmigan hunting throughout their range. One day you might find 50 birds in a willow-choked creekbottom, blueberry patch or a rocky slope at the edge of a snowbank; the next day you can't find a single bird anywhere in the area.

THE LOWER 48: WHITE-TAILED PTARMIGAN

Whitetails are the lone ptarmigan species found in the lower 48 states, and Colorado is without doubt the best state for hunting them. Their favorite feeding and loafing locales are in boulder fields and scree patches at the base of receding snowbanks. Here they dine on nutritious, newly emerging alpine plants along with any available insect-type protein that hops or crawls around.

The most effective way to hunt white-tailed ptarmigan is with several buddies spread out to

White-tailed ptarmigan hunting will take you to some very steep and rocky places. Put on your climbing boots! When you flush a covey, mark where some of the individual birds land, then move in for the re-flush.

and freeze in position, becoming part of the landscape, rendering themselves extremely difficult to pick out.

When you locate birds, back off and summon your partners for a concerted approach. During the fall hunting season, ptarmigan are generally bunched up, so locating a single bird usually means that more birds are nearby. Be conscious of wind direction when you move in for the flush; stiff breezes are common in the mountains and on the tundra, and these feathered bombshells are masters at using the wind to their advantage. They'll want to fly off with the wind.

When a covey is busted, keep your eyes open and mark where the individual birds land. They will generally stay very close to that spot, so you have a chance to make follow-up flushes. But don't be surprised if a spooked flock rockets down the mountain for half a mile or more before putting down; they can be unpredictable.

Ptarmigan are ideal birds to hunt with a dog as they would rather sit tight than run or fly. Watching a good pointing or flushing dog working ptarmigan above timberline on the open tundra during a clear fall day, under a brilliant blue sky with the fall colors blazing and a view that's indescribable, is a hunt every bird hunter should experience.

ALASKA: WILLOW PTARMIGAN

The techniques for hunting the Alaska bush and tundra for willow ptarmigan is much the same as white-tailed methods. The willow ptarmigan scattered throughout this vast state can be found just about anywhere. It can be frustrating

cover a large area. Keep your eyes open for fresh droppings and tracks in the dirt of gopher mounds and mole tunnels; the birds love to dust in such places.

Move slowly through the area, watching closely for slight movement in or around rocky outcroppings or islands. Use a pair of binoculars to glass likely ptarmigan areas from a distance, trying to spot birds while they are still actively moving and feeding. Once ptarmigan see or sense anything they perceive as threatening they'll hunker down

Shotguns & Loads for Ptarmigan

I've probably taken more ptarmigan with bow and arrow while big game hunting than by any other method. Rocky ptarmigan habitat is tough on arrows and especially broadheads, so I generally carry a supply of rubber bludgeon blunts or judo points with me when I'm bowhunting in ptarmigan territory.

The ptarmigan's penchant for holding tight and letting its natural camouflage protect it makes it an ideal target for a .22 pistol or rifle loaded with shorts. This gun's packability and minimal noise also makes a .22 pistol the ideal companion on a big game rifle or bow hunt in ptarmigan country, providing it's legal in your hunting area.

Once convinced of impending danger, a ptarmigan can blow out of a rock pile or willow thicket and rocket down a mountainside or

The traditional grouse shotgun works on ptarmigan too! The author prefers a fast-shooting 20 gauge loaded with No. 7½ shot.

zigzag through the brush in a blur, presenting a tough shotgunning challenge. My shotgun preferences run to a quick-pointing 20 gauge with a field/target load of 7/8 to 1 ounces of 7½ shot, or a 12 gauge loaded with fast target/field or dove shells consisting of 1⅛ ounces of No. 7½s or 6s.

All ptarmigan like to hold tight, preferring to let camouflage, instead of flight, protect them from predators. In situations like this (left), a .22 pistol makes for some great hunting fun. The author takes many ptarmigan with bow-and-arrow (above) during the course of archery hunts for big game: a pleasant (and great-tasting) diversion!

hunting them as you can spend several hours wandering through likely looking cover without seeing a feather. When you've just about had all the fun you can stand—with burned-up leg muscles from slogging through the boggy, foot-sucking tundra and sore, aching ankles from twisting and rolling on the ball-bearing-like gravel and rocks hidden under the mossy vegetation—you stumble over a knob and find yourself in the middle of several hundred of the splotch-patterned birds.

Ptarmigan hunting in Alaska is a long-term venture with the season extending, in all but one area, from early August through March and into April, depending on the unit. Several of the most remote units are open from August through mid-June with a daily limit of 50 birds and 100 in possession. All the areas have liberal bag limits ranging from 10 to 40 birds per day with double the daily limit in possession.

If you are looking for a unique bird hunt, spring ptarmigan hunting from a snowmobile, snowshoes, or cross-country skis might just be the ticket. Many Alaska residents utilize ptarmigan for subsistence and resort to snaring them. One account written many years ago tells of using a pile of gravel to attract driven birds under a drop net. Sounds effective, but I'll stick to a bow, handgun or shotgun for hunting this intriguing little grouse of the tundra.

BIRD OF THE TUNDRA

Ptarmigan hunting is special for many reasons, but one of the most compelling is just being out in the bird's remote tundra home—whether it's an alpine meadow at timberline or a scrubby willow thicket in the far northern wilderness.

Willow ptarmigan hunting will take you to a land of wide vistas and huge expanses. The birds are out there somewhere. Put on your hiking boots!

Finding Ptarmigan

The best ptarmigan hunting state in the Lower 48 is Colorado, with its miles and miles of prime alpine tundra ptarmigan habitat and light hunting pressure. The season generally opens September 1st and runs through mid-November concurrent with most of the fall hunting seasons. The limit is 3 birds daily and 6 in possession.

Corona Pass between Rocky Mountain National Park and Berthoud Pass, Guanella Pass above Georgetown and the Alpine Loop, a 45-mile four-wheel-drive road above Silverton and Ouray, are all excellent places to find white-tailed ptarmigan in huntable numbers.

Without a doubt Alaska is the ptarmigan hunter's paradise, with most of the vast state being prime ptarmigan habitat. In Alaska it's possible to find all three kinds of ptarmigan on one mountain but separated by altitudinal variations. Several outfitters in Alaska specialize in ptarmigan hunting; hunts are conducted with pointing dogs on the wide-open tundra and rock-strewn slopes and ridges. One outfitter I know will even take you on a ptarmigan hunt using trained falcons. Contact the Alaska Department of Fish & Game (907-465-4190) for a listing of guides and outfitters that specialize in ptarmigan hunting or include it in their hunting or fishing package.

Regardless of the main species you're planning to hunt in Alaska or the provinces of northern Canada, do your homework and plan a couple days for some fast-and-furious ptarmigan hunting. You won't be sorry.

Not many hunters can say they've shot a ptarmigan. They're fun birds to hunt, whether as a sidelight to a big game hunt, or on a special trip focused especially on this tundra grouse.

Ptarmigan hunting gives you the chance to bag a white game bird (white-tailed ptarmigan, left). Ptarmigan are attractive in their russet autumn plumage too (willow ptarmigan, right).

Chapter 8

SAGE GROUSE: THE WEST'S BIG GAME BIRD

BY CHRIS MADSON

N o matter how you look at them, sage grouse are spectacular birds. They're North America's largest native grouse—a mature male can weigh up to 7 pounds, more than twice the size of a ring-necked pheasant. During spring courtship, this bruiser is dressed as flamboyantly as any wood duck drake. His costume reminds me a little of Mae West in her heyday: an outlandish headdress of black plumes, a white feather boa around his neck, two voluptuous expanses of bare skin below his neckline, and the trademark shoulders-back, chest-out swagger.

Sage grouse are spectacular birds (cocks will weigh up to 7 pounds) found in spectacular country—the West's biggest, widest places. During hunting season, sage grouse look like the bird at far left. If you get to sage grouse country in spring, you might see cocks (left) strutting, dancing, displaying and competing for hens on traditional, communal breeding grounds known as leks.

This plumage is intended to beguile the ladies and intimidate rivals in the continent's largest courtship gatherings. Sage grouse have taken the prairie grouse custom of communal courtship to its outer limit. In the 1940s, after sage grouse numbers had been decimated by prolonged overgrazing, the gathering of the clans was still an amazing sight. One researcher of the time estimated that more than 400 cocks were present on one Wyoming strutting ground. Another biologist figured that more than 800 cocks and hens attended the spring festivities on one ground in northwest Colorado.

TIMES OF PLENTY

These observations are only a faint echo of the flocks of sage grouse that occupied the basins of the West before they were settled by humans. The Native American name for the upper Green River was *Seedskadee agie*—sage grouse river. When the ornithologist John Townsend came over South Pass into the Green River country in 1834, he reported sage grouse "in flocks of packs, of fifteen or twenty, and so exceedingly tame as to allow an approach to within a few feet, running before our horses like domestic fowl. When we first saw them, the temptation to shoot was irresistible; the guns were cracking all around us."

In 1886, the conservationist George Bird Grinnell camped at the base of a high bluff in Wyoming's Bates Hole. It turned out to be a favorite watering place of the local sage grouse.

"Looking up from the tent at the edge of the bluff above us," Grinnell wrote, "we could see projecting over it the heads of hundreds of the birds, and as those standing there took flight, others stepped forward to occupy their places. The number of Grouse which flew over the camp reminded me of the oldtime flights of Passenger Pigeons that I used to see when I was a boy. Before long the narrow valley where the water was, was a moving mass of gray."

On another hunt, Grinnell and a friend took a day to hunt sage grouse. "The birds seemed to become more numerous as we approached the main stream. At last, when we reached the creek and sat down to rest and count our birds, we found John's bag to consist of 17 sage grouse, 2 ducks, 1 ruffed grouse, and the little beaver. I had

not done quite so well, having only 16 sage grouse, 2 ducks and a snow goose. As we were gathering up our game we heard a faint shout, and turning saw Jack and Jim hastening toward us. They were fairly loaded down with birds, and in answer to our inquiries produced 12 mallards and black ducks, 21 sage grouse, 3 ruffed grouse, and 5 blue-winged teal." That's 54 sage grouse among 4 hunters on foot armed with blackpowder scatterguns.

At the turn of the 20th century, naturalist Leonard Burnett reported even faster shooting among the settlers along the upper Green River. Mounted and armed with modern shotguns and equipped with an intimate knowledge of sage grouse habits, "a single hunter has been known to kill a hundred birds a day without the aid of a dog," according to Burnett.

MODERN SAGE GROUSE HUNTING

Sage grouse have come on hard times since those high, wild days. The species has disappeared from the fringe of its range in northern Arizona and New Mexico, western Kansas and Nebraska, and southern British Columbia. There are probably fewer than 500 birds left in Alberta and Saskatchewan, and the bird has been declared "threatened" by the state of Washington. One biologist has estimated that there are about 157,000 sage grouse left, occupying about half of the bird's former range.

As the bird's name implies, sage grouse are seldom found far from extensive stands of sagebrush. It is a staple of their diet through much of the year, and provides cover in every season. The sagebrush grasslands east of Montana's Continental Divide still support reasonable numbers of sage grouse, and the sagebrush basins of Wyoming are still the stronghold of the species.

Cock sage grouse dance and display on a traditional lek. Civilization's endless war on sage has severely depleted the shrub, and hence sage grouse habitat.

Understanding Sage Grouse

*T*he sage grouse year starts with a dance. Beginning in late February or early March, adult males rendezvous on traditional strutting grounds to establish territories and dominance. In April, the hens begin to visit the strutting grounds, and the most dominant cocks breed with them.

The hens retire to the sage to choose nest sites and begin clutches. A typical clutch has seven eggs. The hen doesn't start incubating until she has finished laying, so all the eggs hatch within a few hours of each other.

Like the young of most other chicken-like game birds, the sage grouse chick is ready to follow its mother away from the nest within hours of hatching. Most clutches hatch in the last half of May, and the young birds grow explosively on a diet of insects. By the time they are 2 weeks old, the youngsters can make short flights.

Always sociable except when they are tending nests, the birds begin to gather in flocks in early fall. Sage grouse summering in the foothills often have more water and better cover, but they pay for these comforts

A cock displays on a lek. Hens choose the biggest, best and most impressive dancers, and mate only with them.

with a substantial migration to lower elevation in late fall.

Strong fliers, these birds might fly for miles at altitudes of 200 to 500 feet. In a bad winter, sage grouse might move 50 miles or more to places where sagebrush stands above the snow, offering a vital combination of forage and cover. Flocks of adult males tend to winter in areas with deeper snow; hens and young birds move to lower elevations where conditions are milder.

A recent decision by the American Ornithological Union has created a new species of sage grouse, the Gunnison's sage grouse. These birds are slightly smaller than other sage grouse and show some differences in plumage and courtship behavior. Found only in western Colorado, the Gunnison's sage grouse has been proposed as an endangered species—there are probably fewer than 3,000 of these birds left in the wild. An estimated 150,000 "greater" sage grouse live in the bird's remaining range.

A sage grouse hen is well camouflaged for her habitat.

Sage grouse range.

Grass is an important component of good sage grouse habitat, and where it mixes with sage (left), you have the makings of excellent sage grouse cover. Water (right) completes the picture. When snow isn't on the ground, sage grouse need standing water to drink.

There is probably more public access to good sage grouse cover in Wyoming than anywhere else on the continent.

Recognizing good sage grouse cover can be challenging. To the casual eye, sage grouse country seems to be an endless monotype of blue-gray shrubbery. Actually, there are differences that can be vitally important to both the grouse and grouse hunters.

Find Mixed Cover

Through spring and summer into early fall, sage grouse need a mix of grass and forbs with their sage. Researchers have found that most sage grouse hens nest under a sagebrush plant, but they are far more likely to bring off their broods if they also have a screen of grass or other broadleafed plants to help them hide from predators.

After they hatch, the chicks need a high-protein diet to support their explosive growth. For the first three weeks of their lives, the young birds subsist almost entirely on insects. The hen needs a little protein as well since she goes through a molt as the chicks are growing.

Bugs do better in a mix of grass, forbs and shrubs than they do in sagebrush alone, so the health and productivity of a sage grouse population is tied to the variety and abundance of the "understory" in a stand of sage. Take a look below the sage—if other stuff grows down there, your chances of finding sage grouse improve.

Find Water

A second key component of good sage grouse cover is water. Sage country is high, cold desert; the things that live here have adapted to that harsh fact. During the winter, sage grouse can get the water they need from snow. It's not unusual for a flock of sage hens to continue visiting a snow bank through the spring until it disappears.

During late spring and early summer, the birds get much of the water they need from dew, moisture left on leaves by passing thundershowers, or the water content of forage itself. However, as the summer passes and water becomes hard to find, sage grouse will visit a spring, creek or stock tank on into fall. In dry years, large flocks are drawn to any surface water that remains; in exceptionally wet years, the birds will be more scattered.

Work with radioed sage grouse suggests that, during the dry periods of late summer and fall, the birds spend most of their time within a mile of a waterhole. They come in to drink before dawn or at dusk, sometimes in large numbers.

A Little Agriculture Helps

As a general rule, sage grouse don't take kindly to the plow. The loss of large areas of sage inevitably leads to a loss of grouse. However, small patches of irrigated alfalfa or clover in large expanses of sage do attract sage grouse in late summer and fall.

The simplest tactic for finding sage grouse,

then, is to gain access to a privately owned hay field in the middle of a huge tract of sage. The toughest part of this approach is getting permission from the landowner, who probably has a long line of friends and relations ready to help him with any sage grouse depredation problems he may be having.

Such fields can attract large numbers of birds of all ages. According to Bob Patterson, the man who literally wrote the book on Wyoming sage grouse, adult cocks and barren hens abandon hay fields after they've been shot at once or twice, but broods linger in these areas and absorb most of the gunning pressure as a result.

If you want to narrow down a huge sweep of sage grouse habitat into one chunk that has a better chance of producing birds, start near the water. Research suggests you'll find fall birds within a mile of a waterhole; those are pretty good odds when you look at how far away a sage grouse country horizon is.

Shotguns & Loads for Sage Grouse

The sage grouse is a big bird, but because of its heavy wing loading and thin skin, it is easier to knock down than a goose of the same size or even a large duck like the mallard. Modern pheasant gauges, loads and chokes are generally adequate. For me, that means a 12 gauge choked improved cylinder shooting a 1¼- to 1⅜-ounce load of 6s.

Since sage grouse generally hold reasonably well, you can get away with smaller chokes and lighter loads than this if you are a good shot and show restraint in the shots you take. But before you decide to use your 28 gauge, bear in mind this comment from a hunter in 1904: "Another objectionable feature is their ability to carry off shot, which borders on the marvelous. A light gun, deadly on other grouse, will hardly serve for these big fellows."

A 12 gauge filled with 1¼ to 1⅜ ounces of No. 6 shot makes a good sage grouse combo. Make it a gun you can carry all day. Choke it loosely—improved-cylinder is good.

Hunting Strategies & Tactics

If you aren't blessed with a doting uncle who raises alfalfa in the Wyoming sage, you'll probably find yourself hunting the public domain. The sensible way to hunt these huge tracts of sage is to check stock ponds, creeks and irrigation impoundments for sage grouse sign. If you find reasonably fresh tracks or droppings, work the surrounding uplands systematically for half a mile or more in every direction. Coulees with a combination of grasses, forbs and sage might be a little better than the drier uplands, though not always.

Look for heads as you work the cover—sage grouse are big birds, and they aren't afraid to sneak a peek at an approaching noise. It's not unusual to see several heads bobbing up and down in the brush ahead as you walk. And if you flush one bird, be ready for more. Sage grouse are sociable, typically moving in groups of half a dozen or more. They often flush in ones or twos

and might even give you time to reload before they clear out.

With the screen of shrubbery reaching endlessly in every direction, you'd think sage grouse would be the ultimate runners. Suprisingly, they're not. Maybe they've learned that it's pointless to try to outrun a coyote, that they're better off gambling that he'll walk by and then fly if he doesn't. Whatever the reason, they might move a little to get into taller cover, but they'll often hunker down once they get into sagebrush that's tall enough to cover them. This means they hold better for a pointing dog than many other desert birds will—certainly better than the typical corn-stubble pheasant.

Whether you use a pointer or flusher, a dog with good retrieving skills is a blessing on a sage grouse hunt. You might spend a couple of hard hours hiking the brush before you see any birds. If you're hunting without a dog, you'll be wise to mark the first bird you shoot and walk over to

As you hunt sage grouse, look for heads popping up above the sage for a peek at your approach. Surprisingly, the birds won't run forever. If a couple birds flush and you happen to miss, or hit one and your dog is on the case, reload right away because some birds will always hold a little longer. Move on in for these second and third flushes.

him without taking your eyes off the spot, regardless of how many other birds flush.

A sage grouse is a big pile of feathers, but he's colored to blend with the cover. If you take a second shot, you'll be amazed at how difficult your first bird is to find. If you have a good retriever, however, you can take full advantage of the covey when it rises, secure in the knowledge that the dog shouldn't have too much trouble finding several pounds of dead grouse if you get him somewhere in the neighborhood.

Before you pull the trigger,

A bomber is a big, mature male sage grouse. He takes off slowly and in a lumbering manner, and on the table tastes like sage brush. What you want to shoot are the smallest, youngest birds (and the fastest flyers). They're the best eating.

Dogs for Sage Grouse

A good dog is a distinct advantage during a sage grouse hunt. If you're used to working a dog in more temperate climates, be prepared for a little disappointment—the scenting conditions in sagebrush desert during the shirtsleeve days of September are about as bad as they could be anywhere. The dry air retains little scent, and the constant wind disperses what little scent there is in a matter of moments.

A dog is invaluable in sage grouse country, if for nothing else than another set of legs to get birds moving. Bring along plenty of water for your canine assistant.

If you expect any decent work out of your dog, carry water for him. In these circumstances, he'll be needing a sip at least every 20 minutes. You'll also need plenty of water for yourself.

The obvious advantage of a dog in these stands of featureless cover is that he extends your range. Even if he doesn't trail the birds, he will probably get them to move. If he doesn't see them walking ahead, you might.

you should know one other thing. For generations, westerners have done their best to avoid shooting adult male sage grouse, known as "bombers" for their size and lumbering take-off. The largest cocks are at least 2 years old, and they are the "sagiest" of all sage grouse on the table.

The real prize is the bird of the year, 3 months old, about the size of its mother, tender and mild. If you have a taste for ducks, a sage grouse of any age is palatable enough, but if you're leery of dark meat, you might want to sharpen your ability to pick the youngsters out of a flock.

LOOKING TO THE HORIZON

Sage grouse numbers have always gone through booms and busts, and the pattern has become more pronounced as the species has declined. Some observers believe the fluctuations reflect a 10-year cycle in grouse populations, but there's no evidence of any mechanism that might cause a regular rise and fall in their numbers. Changes in sage grouse abundance are probably driven by weather.

Drought has the most powerful influence. Sagebrush is well equipped to survive extended drought, but many of the grasses and forbs in the sage aren't as tough. A reduction in stands of these plants reduces cover for hens and their broods, and decimates insect populations in the bargain. A dry year means a drastic drop in sage grouse production, as it does with desert quail in the Southwest.

Roads for development purposes put a big squeeze on sage grouse habitat.

Sage grouse have come on hard times over the last century. Some people have suggested closing sage grouse seasons to protect the bird. But the problem isn't hunting. The trouble lies in the

It will be up to hunters to save sage grouse, which means saving sage grouse habitat. Hunt this magnificent bird in the wide open spaces he calls home, and you will understand the allure.

sagebrush country itself and in our treatment of it. Persistent overgrazing, rampant oil and gas drilling, the games we've played with Western water, plowing and subdividing the land have all contributed to the downward slide of one of America's great game birds.

There's still time to reverse the trends in the sage, but someone must take a personal interest. When wildlife has faced problems in the past, that "someone" has always been a hunter. He starts out looking for a target and ends up building an allegiance to a piece of country. I hope our pursuit of the sage grouse will lead us to re-examine our relationship with the sagebrush wilderness, the least appreciated of all our wild places.

Finding Sage Grouse

This is what you'll see: a gray ghost slinking through the sage and grass.

The best of what's left for sage grouse hunters is in Wyoming and Montana, but sage grouse seasons are also open in Oregon, California, Nevada, Idaho, Utah and Colorado. The number of permits issued for the birds is limited in Oregon and California.

Hunter's should also note that open seasons for bombers are becoming even shorter. California's season is now two days long; Colorado's is one week. Even in Wyoming, widely regarded as the heart of sage grouse country, the season only lasts 16 days. Montana is the sole exception to this trend—their season still lasts from September 1 through the end of November.

Montana biologists offer a simple defense for this liberal season: they don't believe that hunting has anything to do with fluctuations in sage grouse numbers. They're probably right.

For generations, sage grouse seasons have begun in late summer, giving hunters the chance to take young birds soon after they could fly and when they were best on the table. Research indicates that hens with chicks are more likely to be shot than adult hens and cocks on their own. The loss of the hen then affects the survival of the scattered young. Based on this reasoning, many states have delayed their season openers until mid-September, allowing broods to break up on their own before the shooting starts.

Sage grouse hunting is about being there, out in the "big wide open" that is the true West.

Chapter 9

SHARPTAILS: CHASING THE PRAIRIE GROUSE

By Mark Kayser

Sharptails live in a large and lonely land, and that is part of their attraction. Plus, the birds are beautiful to behold (far left). They are also admirable because they are tough as nails (left), surviving a harsh prairie winter just fine.

*I*t takes a special breed to live and survive out West. Judging from the numbers of humans populating the Great Plains and Western prairies, few souls have the hardiness to battle the extremes of desert-like summers and tundra-like winters.

The same goes for the animals that inhabit the rolling sage, grasslands and river breaks. They've adapted to the extremes: temperatures that rise above 100°F and crash to minus 40; winds that howl at more than 60 mph; and drought-stricken landscapes where water flat-out disappears.

Yet, when nature releases this wrath of open country weather, the native species suffer surprisingly little.

Sharp-tailed grouse are one of those hardy natives like mighty bison and the sharp-eyed pronghorn. Because of this hardiness, sharptails have managed to inhabit a good portion of the Northern Hemisphere. Although the Great Plains and Western real estate is where most hunters meet up with the cackling native, sharptail distribution extends through most Canadian provinces and into Alaska's interior. They may be found in a gentle, rolling creekbottom or at the top of a

Understanding Sharptails

*T*ympanuchus phasianellus, or the sharp-tailed grouse, has been around since the Pleistocene epoch when mammoths wandered with the sharptails. Tales of huge sharptail flocks numbering in the hundreds, if not thousands, were commonplace from the first explorers and pioneers invading the Great Plains and Western prairies. Pioneers hunting for food, expanding agricultural practices and overgrazing have all combined to severely restrict sharptail density within their range. But because of their adaptability to withstand some agricultural intrusion, sharptails have not totally disappeared from their range and have survived in smaller flocks inhabiting niche areas.

Sharptails measure approximately 15 inches in length and weigh less than 2 pounds. Both sexes look similar in color with a brown backside and a lighter, almost-white belly. Chest feathers have a telltale brown "V-shape" checkering as compared to the prairie chicken, which has brown horizontal bars on its chest.

It's not uncommon for early-season prairie grouse hunters to bag the occasional immature pheasant by mistake because of the birds' similar coloring. When bearing down on a flushing bird, look for a white underbelly and listen for a telltale cackle (a "chuk-chuk-chuk-chuk") before pulling the trigger. My hunting partners make it a rule to yell "hen" or "grouse" when being joined by first-time grousers.

A closer inspection reveals that sharptails sport custom snowshoes with their feathered feet. The five-inch pointed tail finishes the sharptails' major distinguishing characteristic. Its tail is much shorter

A sharptail cock will dance on his spot on a lek (breeding display ground), competing with other cocks for the available hens.

than a pheasant's, but is not rounded like a prairie chicken's.

When spooked, a sharptail flock will take off quickly, but hunters should be prepared for the occasional straggler or two. Fleeing distance of the flock depends on how many times the birds have been pressured. I've seen some flocks fly less than 300 yards before landing, but many flocks fly out of sight. For optimum distance, they use an alternating glide and wing beat combination. Be sure to follow through with your aim since sharptails have a habit of rocking back and forth in flight.

Sharptails are attracted to high quality foods, with grains of choice being wheat, corn and millet. In true grasslands, they depend on buds, berries, twigs and rose hips. Early in the fall and especially in the summer, sharptails occasionally munch on insects but the bulk of their intake centers on plant material.

Roosting cover consists of grasslands or CRP fields. Morning finds sharptails leaving their roosting cover before daylight and targeting a food source. After feeding, they search for grit and moisture, then return to grassy areas for rest and relaxation. At the end of the day they'll feed again before returning to roost at dark.

Sharptails mate in March and April. Hens and cocks gather at leks, traditional breeding grounds where cocks dance and meet ready hens. Hens nest in April and May in the proximity of the dancing ground. If you ever have the chance to witness the spring mating rituals of prairie grouse species like sharptails, prairie chickens or sage grouse, don't miss the spectacle!

Sharptail range.

mountain speckled with immature pines.

This variety is what makes sharptail hunting so addictive to the upland game enthusiast. But one quality encompasses all the sharptail's habitats: vastness. Sharptail country is big. From eastern Montana's river breaks to the prairies of southern Saskatchewan to the Sandhills of western Nebraska, sharptails inhabit country with a big view and plenty of room to break in a new pair of boots.

The sharptail is a survivor. Even so, one is not perched atop every corner post or hidden behind every bush. Many a fanatic upland game hunter has traveled out West to shoot a brace of sharptails only to return with a worn-out pair of boots and a full supply of ammunition.

Remember that a sharptail likes to see what's going on: He prefers living in short grass he can peek over, and he likes hilltops and ridgetops.

FINDING SHARPTAILS

Sharptail habitat varies widely. But specific land features, food sources and vegetative habitat can lure birds into preferred pockets that you can identify. To thwart blisters and save on boot leather, it pays to take a few notes on the preferred habitats of these prairie ghosts.

I was raised in South Dakota, where upland bird hunting was as mandatory as kindergarten.

And even though the wily ringneck often took precedence, the sharptail holds the number one spot in my upland outing Daytimer. After years of hunting with some of the best pioneers in the prairie grouse community, I've noted many of their favorite haunts to target for sharptails. Today, my boots still get a workout. But at least they last a full season before the leather succumbs to the dry, cutting edge of prairie rocks and cactus.

It's About the Weather

Sharptails reside in various locations due to one main factor: the weather. Since many sharptail hunting seasons begin in early fall and extend into wintry weather months, sharptail hunting locales change whenever the Weather Channel reports an approaching front.

Sharptails have a few stringent rules they follow, regardless of the weather.

• First, sharptails like to be able to see. When they're not feeding, sharptails often rest on high ridges. They prefer to peer from areas with short grass that's just high enough for concealment. In winter, they also perch high, or sit in the tops of trees, again allowing for superb surveillance.

• Second, sharptails fly almost everywhere and are not afraid to travel great distances.

• Finally, sharptails reside in flocks; where there's one bird, get ready for more.

Most of my sharptail hunting takes place during the early season—mainly in September. While September signals the beginning of fall, don't be fooled. In the open country of the Great Plains and Western states, temperatures hover between 80°F to 100°F. Critters can't help but be affected. During these conditions, sharptails stray slightly from their routine: As temperatures rise, sharptails abandon their high-top ridges for shade in brushy draws and overgrown slopes. Nearby water also lures birds. Shade plus water equals birds on a hot day.

Abundant early-season feed means that birds don't have to fly miles to a grain field. Grain fields

In early season when the weather is hot, you'll often have to head to brush and shade, where the sharptails go to cool off.

near sharptail habitat lure birds throughout the season, so don't overlook them. In the heart of the fall, sharptails follow a standard procedure of feeding in available grain fields at sunrise and loafing on high ridges or roosting atop old barns and trees throughout the day. Finally, as winter brings upon its beastly attitude, sharptails begin traveling extreme distances between ideal roosting and feeding areas, again using stubble grain fields if available.

HUNTING SHARPTAILS

I really can't recall the number of times I've fielded this question: "I've been hunting the Fort Pierre National Grasslands for two days and haven't shot a sharptail yet. What am I doing wrong?"

The Fort Pierre National Grasslands is just one of many good public areas for sharptails and greater prairie chickens. But the grasslands include 116,000 acres of grass. That's like searching for a couple dozen needles in a haystack. Your odds have improved, but not by much.

To hunt sharptails successfully, you need to follow three basic rules. First, hunt areas sharptails prefer as outlined in the previous paragraphs. Second, hunt with a dog—either a retriever or a

Shotguns & Loads for Sharptails

A good friend of mine says that sharptails give up too easy. Sometimes it's hard to disagree with his assumption. It's not that sharptails are easy to hit with their pheasant-style eruption. Rather, it simply doesn't take a whole load to bring them out of the sky. And unlike the snake-like pheasant that crawls under a grass canopy to disappear, whether wounded or not, sharptails sit where they dropped when wounded.

My favorite shotgun for sharptails is the 20 gauge. Early-season coveys flush at stone-throwing distances requiring a modified or improved choke and the use of No. 6 or 7½ shot in a 1-ounce load. Later in the season, when hunting wilder flushing coveys or pass shooting, a full choke may be justified, bumping the load to 1¼ ounce load of No. 5s. Gun choice is personal, but pump and autoloader enthusiasts definitely have opportunities to shoot a limit in a matter of seconds with a slow-rising covey. But even over-and-under aficionados generally have time to reload the pipes as birds gather their senses during a flush. Besides, there's usually a straggler or two in every group.

The author likes a 20 gauge and No. 6 or 7½ shot for sharptails (though your 12 gauge will do), and he is more than happy with a good autoloader (shown) or pump gun.

pointer. Finally, be in good physical shape. Sharptail country is no place to start your January resolution of getting into shape.

First, watch the weather and plan your hunt accordingly. Sharptails switch habitat and patterns depending on weather. Wet weather can greatly restrict travel into out-of-the-way sharptail hot spots.

Don't be afraid to ask locals about the locations of sharptails. Many locals keep pheasant hot spots to themselves but view sharptails as a "ho-hum" species.

Since sharptails generally reside in big flocks that get bigger as the days get colder, they

Early and late in the day, sharptails will feed in grain stubble fields. That's where you want to be hunting when the sun is rising or descending.

are noticeable. Bring binoculars and glass the horizon. (I don't know how many times I've surprised prairie newcomers by glassing for moving flocks of sharptails.) Once you jump a flock, watch where they go. After they land, sharptails don't have the running tendency of a rooster pheasant, but will usually stay put, or waddle into cover that is close by.

Early in the fall, sharptail flocks consist of young-of-the year birds or the college freshmen squad. But after being hotly pursued by pointers and retrievers, these freshmen quickly acquire a doctorate in survival and flush as wildly as any cagey rooster in the Dakotas. I've hunted flocks near my hometown that I couldn't get close to even if I wore a ghillie-style suit and crawled up on them. On the other hand, I've hunted flocks in remote Montana locales that allowed entrance into their ranks and bowhunting-close kinds of shots.

Dogs & Sharptails

*S*harptail hunting doesn't require a dog, but to save money on yet another pair of boots, bring one.

Most breeds of hunting dogs work for sharptails. In my home state of South Dakota, Labradors are as common as cowboy hats, and everyone uses a Lab to hunt prairie grouse. The only drawback to a Lab is trying to hunt a black one in the extreme heat of early-season hunts. Speaking of heat, never take off on an open-country trek without water for you and your four-legged hunting companion. Few sharptails reside in water-rich country.

My favorite sharptail breeds are wide-ranging pointers like Brittanys, English setters and German shorthairs. Labs can definitely cover country, but by their nature, they stay close for flushing action. Flushing dogs prove their worth late in the season when jumpy birds require a close-ranging dog.

Pointers trained on the prairie can really cover country. Good pointers race across the prairie like wildfire. In pastures covering thousands of acres, a

A good dog will save you a lot of steps in the search for birds ... and bring back the ones you drop.

dog that covers country will find the widely scattered hideouts of sharptails. Conditioning of any dog used for sharptails should begin a minimum of a month in advance of the hunt or the season.

And don't kick the dog out for a solo run and follow behind in the SUV. Personal physical training should rank right up there with dog conditioning. When you're running the dog, run or walk yourself. Sharptail country is no place to discover personal shortcomings. Walk in the boots you plan to hunt in, and (within reason) don't avoid training on hot days, because September temperatures mirror summer's heat.

Special Strategies

As the weather cools, flock size increases and the dummies have long since gone home in someone's cooler. Leftover birds require strategy. Watch where they roost and decide whether the cover is tall enough for a dog to approach for a flush. If not, watch their feeding pattern. Can you approach them in the stubble or brushy areas as they feed? Finally, if stalking or flushing approaches look dismal, does pass shooting present an option? Do they fly a traceable pattern between feeding and roosting areas?

Sharptail country—big, rugged, bold, seemingly endless—is a wonderful place to walk, to hunt, to just breathe the fresh and clean air.

Keep all these tips in mind as well. Sharptails don't hole up in heavy cover like most upland species. They prefer to be high, watching for danger. A major exception is hot weather when they seek shade. If it's windy they still sit high, but can be found on the leeward side of the hill. Unfortunately, like many species sitting in wind, they get jumpy and fly at the mere hint of danger, whether it is real or not.

A SPECIAL BREED

Sharptails truly are a special breed—a prairie native that survives, even thrives, in a hot-cold-wet-dry-rugged-tough land of extremes. And it takes a special breed of hunter to love sharptails: someone willing to walk the big country and put in time searching the land for these wonderful birds.

Finding Sharptails

With sharptails spread across a large geographic area, sharptail hunters have many good hunting choices in hunting locales. Sharptails reside in parts or all of Alaska, the Yukon, eastern British Columbia, Alberta, Saskatchewan, Manitoba, western Ontario, Quebec, Montana, Idaho, Utah, Washington, North Dakota, South Dakota, Wyoming, Kansas, Colorado, Wisconsin, Upper Michigan, Minnesota and Nebraska.

Hunters traditionally focus on sharptails in the following prime areas: Saskatchewan, Manitoba, Montana, North Dakota, South Dakota and Nebraska. Not only are population densities greater here, but these regions also provide opportunities for combination hunts with other species like pheasants, Hungarian partridge, greater prairie chickens, sage grouse and waterfowl. Although sharptails make any trip across the county or country worthwhile, the bonus of a combination hunt is icing on the prairie game bird cake.

Chapter 10

PRAIRIE CHICKENS: WALKING THE TALL GRASS

BY MARK KAYSER

Although the cow and the plow have severely depleted prairie chicken habitat, the birds enjoy a few prairie strongholds yet. A few serious upland hunters come out to chase chickens every year, searching the tall grass for one of the handsome birds (far left). You can distinguish a prairie chicken (left) from a sharptail by its pinnated neck feathers, distinctly barred chest, and square tail feathers in flight.

Sometimes it's hard to see the uniqueness in something you encounter daily. For instance, some folks have bird feeders attracting blue jays, grosbeaks, chickadees and finches. My South Dakota bird feeder attracts a different crowd. Visitors include ring-necked pheasants, sharptailed grouse, mule deer and, probably the most unique guest of all, the greater prairie chicken.

To my family, the everyday appearance of the "chickens" doesn't even raise an eyebrow, except when the flock occasionally roosts on my son's backyard swing set. Yet even after seeing the chickens daily, I have to take a moment to admire the gutsy, pinnated birds as they buck hurricane-style prairie winds for a bellyful of grain.

Most upland enthusiasts don't look at the prairie chicken with that same "ho-hum" attitude. This hardy prairie native ranks as one of the top upland trophies for the traveling wing shooter. To many hunters, chicken hunting is a pilgrimage, not just a trip. They don't come to the prairie for a possession limit, or even a daily limit like most pheasant hunters. They're here to capture the moment when their pointing dog locks up on a snootful of chicken and they brush past the dog for a front row flushing spectacle.

I've helped many hunters get their chickens. I can't remember how many of those birds have gone to the taxidermist but, needless to say, business is steady for chicken taxidermy work in chicken country.

Understanding Prairie Chickens

For those of you versed in Latin, the greater prairie chicken's scientific name, *tympanuchus cupido*, sounds more like a dinosaur. With many species invading the prairie due to man's alterations, the prairie chicken may indeed be a dinosaur in a changing world.

This light brown game bird is distinguishable from sharp-tailed grouse by its black pinnated neck feathers, orange eyebrows and brown barring on its cream-colored chest feathers. The feet are off-yellow in color and not feathered like sharptail feet. In flight, the tail of the prairie chicken looks square. Prairie chickens weigh 2 to 2½ pounds. Their dark-colored meat provides great table fare; many chefs in chicken country marinate the breast meat and grill it like filet mignon.

Chickens explode from cover like pheasants but use a combination wing beat and glide to cover great distances. They can reach aerial speeds of 40 mph. Prairie chickens are vocal and make a soft cluck when flushing, but become very vocal indeed when "booming" on their traditional breeding grounds, called leks, during the spring mating season.

These springtime breeding antics center around a traditional lek that sits on a high prairie overlook. Males and females meet on the lek. Males defend a small territory while dancing and making their booming noises that can carry a mile on clear prairie days. While displaying, male prairie chickens raise their pinnate feathers and inflate orange air sacs on their necks. Booming accompanies this dance routine.

Like other prairie grouse, chickens take care of breeding duty on a communal lek where males dance, make loud "boom" noises, display their bright eye combs and neck patches, and generally carry on for the selective hens.

Prairie chickens feed on a variety of food sources depending on seasonal changes in food and proximity to agriculture. The birds might fly several miles to feed, returning to midday loafing cover (or nighttime roosting cover) when done. Green vegetation, insects, grain, fruit, berries, buds and sprouts make up the largest percentage of a chicken's diet. Find the food source for each period of the fall and you'll find chickens.

Prairie chicken range.

FINDING PRAIRIE CHICKENS

Like the sharp-tailed grouse, prairie chickens once inhabited much of North America's grasslands. Unlike the sharptail, prairie chickens have not been successful in dealing with settlers of European origin.

Agricultural practices destroyed much of the pristine prairie. This alteration brought pheasants to the Great Plains, but caused prairie chicken numbers to decline drastically. And with a more demanding habitat requirement than that of their cousin the sharptail, prairie chicken numbers continue to hinge on federal grasslands and large expanses of native pastures untouched by the plow.

There are two species of prairie chickens: the greater and lesser. Both species are referred to as pinnated grouse due to long neck feathers called pinnates that both males and females possess. The male's pinnates are longer and stand erect during spring courtship displays. The lesser prairie chicken lives in a small region in the arid south central United States. It is the namesake bird—the greater prairie chicken of South Dakota, Nebraska and Kansas—that hunters seek. Throughout the rest of this story, all chicken references refer to the greater prairie chicken.

Good grass—and lots of it—is prairie chicken habitat's key ingredient.

It's About the Grass

Prairie chickens favor many of the same haunts as their native cousins, sharp-tailed grouse. Having evolved in the intercontinental savannah, the prairie chicken favors the tall grass prairie, particularly areas with a mixture of prairie grasses.

With the help of the federal Conservation Reserve Program (CRP), chickens have rebounded in recent years.

Many well-managed native pastures will also hold chickens. Well-managed refers to pastures which receive grazing rotation to maintain a stand of grass, or that have grass left uncut from hay production.

Prairie Chicken Habits

Like most prairie wildlife, prairie chickens use eyesight as their main defense. Because of this, they prefer to sit high when loafing and resting. Ridgetops, hills and even the grades of constructed prairie dugouts provide the needed elevation for a sentry as long as the grass allows for a clear view. Other defenses include good hearing and the intricate camouflage pattern of the feathers.

Sharptails often hang out in shady brush, especially on hot fall days. But prairie chickens rarely seek brush in prairie draws, except in wintry conditions. An ideal prairie chicken hangout would consist of a large, rolling tract of good-quality grass consisting of several thousand acres, adjacent to grainfields.

Having read many novels describing the settlement of the prairie, I wonder how anything ever lived under the extremes of the seasons. Those seasonal extremes dictate the location of chickens in their home playing field.

Summer finds the birds basking in the bounty of insects and green plants, with chicks feeding heavily on insects such as grasshoppers. In the fall, the prairie provides unlimited food sources such as berries, greens, seeds, buds, and grains from surrounding croplands. Winter's arrival might cause chickens to fly extreme distances between roosting and feeding areas. It's not uncommon to see huge flocks of chickens flying several miles from evening roosting cover to morning feeding areas. Winter food sources include tree and shrub buds, grainfields and left-over feed from livestock feeding practices. Prairie chicken movement of more than 50 miles to wintering habitat has been documented. Spring once again brings bountiful food sources to the prairie in the form of fresh greens and insects.

HUNTING PRAIRIE CHICKENS

Prairie chicken seasons vary slightly depending on the state you choose to hunt. All prairie chicken states either start their hunts in mid-September or currently offer an early-season opportunity generally beginning at that time. Most states also offer late-season opportunities. The hunting strategies from September to December vary as much as the temperatures.

Early-Season Strategies

September hunting means shirtsleeves, water bottles and trust in a veteran dog. Don't waste time searching in likely pheasant hideouts or even areas where sharptails might seek escape from the heat. Chickens can be found high and on the

Hunt prairie chickens using the right strategy for the season at hand (early or late), and you're much more likely to end up with a brace of beautiful birds like this.

lookout, peering from hilltop grass that barely conceals the flock.

Don't attack these birds in a full frontal assault. Determine the wind direction and use the knowledge that chickens generally reside on leeward sides of hills, out of the wind. Approach these high points by staying on the windward side as you ascend the ridge. When you near the top of the ridge, slide over the top—angling into the wind for the benefit of the dog—and be prepared for action. If good grass exists, drop the sneaky backside approach, but stay high, searching for birds on prairie hills and ridges.

Besides ridges, grasslands adjacent to grainfields also hold birds. Although chickens exist on

Shotguns & Loads for Prairie Chickens

Early-season prairie chickens generally hold well for dogs, and 20-yard shots are common. The 20 gauge, when outfitted with a modified or improved-cylinder choke and teamed up with a load of 6 or 7½ shot, works well in most early-season hunting applications. A prairie chicken is not particularly hard to kill, and will fall from the sky even when marginally hit.

Many purist wing shooters now consider the 28 gauge to be the premier firearm for this type of birding, but unless you are intimate with the gun, a 20 gauge provides a slightly better alternative. Late-season shooters might want to beef up and use the 12 gauge for pass-shooting and extended flushing shots; No. 5 or 6 shot will offer a better punch when teamed with a full choke for high-flying flocks.

a variety of food sources, grain attracts them throughout the fall and winter. As temperatures begin to drop, the natural tendency of chickens to gather begins, and flocks of 10 to 12 suddenly become 30 to 90 birds. Where sharptails overlap, the flocks become a mixture of chickens and grouse. An interesting note is that male chickens generally live by themselves or in small bachelor coveys. They rejoin the flock during winter and the spring breeding season.

Late-Season Strategies

Approaching a late-season flock takes strategy and luck. Twenty eyes suddenly turn into 60. You might try binoculars and patience. Instead of tackling the prairies, wait for large flocks to ascend on a grainfield, then pass-shoot them during their arrival or departure. In Kansas, hunters have the flocks so well patterned that blinds are built, much like they would be for duck hunting on a marsh. Pass-shooting requires scouting for feeding areas like harvested grainfields or pastures where ranchers might be feeding cattle. Use binoculars, watch for large flocks to converge on the fields, and note the birds' flight plans for future pass-shooting opportunities.

DOG NOTES

Whether you're hunting early or late, a dog definitely increases success in locating coveys and finding crippled birds during a flurry of shooting.

Early-season hunting means hot weather, and hunters need to keep water close at hand to cool the radiators of hard-running dogs. You might need to put boots on your dog if you're hunting new country that can harbor prickly pear cactus or sand burrs.

Pass-shooters get their money out of retrievers when "winged," high-flying chickens occasionally sail to the far side of a field.

VISITING THE PAST

Before man and his plow invaded the pristine prairie, chickens abounded. With an endless sea of grass as their home, these wonderful prairie grouse thrived. Of course, the prairie will never return to what it once was. But with CRP and the foresight to keep land in (or revert it back to) its natural state, we are still graced with the majesty of this great game bird—the prairie chicken—in our midst.

Finding Prairie Chickens

Unlike sharptail hunting, which offers a variety of hunting locations, prairie chicken hunting is limited to South Dakota, Nebraska and Kansas. National grasslands, state managed game production areas and CRP acreages offer prime habitat in which to find chickens. South Dakota's Fort Pierre National Grasslands, South Dakota's Missouri River Breaks, the Nebraska Sandhills and the Flint Hills of Kansas provide the nation's top prairie chicken hunting today. Prairie chicken hunting is not a matter of limits, but revering the undeveloped Great Plains with the possibility of returning home with a trophy.

In most prairie chicken country, you have a good chance of running into sharptails as well (prairie chicken on right, sharptail on left). It's the little "slam" of prairie grouse hunting.

Chapter 11

HUNS: GAME BIRD OF THE STEPPES

BY BEN O. WILLIAMS

*I*ts proper name is gray partridge (*Perdix perdix*), but it is known throughout North America as the Hungarian partridge or just "Hun." The Hun is no longer a strange or secret bird; healthy numbers reside in several states, and in some places hunters harvest very high numbers of birds annually.

To successfully hunt Huns, one has to know the birds' habitat, read the cover, learn the Hun's habits, hunt with a plan, and then know what to do once a covey is flushed.

The names Hun, Hungarian Partridge and Gray Partridge all describe the same imported but important game bird. Huns (far left) have filled an available habitat niche in areas too intensively farmed or grazed for native prairie grouse. That said, some grass (left) is essential for the Hun's well-being.

HUN HABITAT

The first step to hunting Huns is knowing where to find them. Three very different types of habitats will hold Huns.

Agricultural Areas

The gray partridge is native to the steppes—vast semiarid grasslands, savannas and sagebrush plains—of eastern Europe, and central and western Asia. The climate in that part of the world corresponds to the climate the Hun now occupies here in North America. Huns were first introduced in the northern and mid-continental prairies of the United States and Canada around 1900. Though many attempts failed at first, today Huns are well established in the steppes of North America.

Classic Hun terrain includes: flat crop fields dissected by creekbottoms and clumps of thickets; grainfields with brushy draws; and sagebrush knolls with food and cover. These are Hun havens, but you don't necessarily need crop fields to have a good partridge population.

Understanding the Hungarian Partridge

Gray partridge have been able to adapt to a great variety of food. Food for Huns comes from four primary sources: seeds of various weedy herbs, cultivated grains, green leafy material and insects.

Spring foods consist of a large amount of tender leaves, blades of grass, waste grain, weed seeds gleaned from fields, and a few insects when available. The young feed mostly on insects during their growth period, and later turn to green plants. The fall and winter diet in farmed regions is mainly cereal grains (like wheat) where available, but greens are still consumed. In grasslands with no grainfields present, weed seeds are consumed in place of cereal grains. During winter, if grainfields are fairly close to grasslands, prairie Huns will travel a considerable distance to feed in these fields, but these are temporary feeding places and are not essential.

Huns do not need free water to live. Water requirements are met by heavy dews, insects, seeds and greens. Birds will concentrate along brushy draws and low seepage areas where free water is available, but they don't necessarily use it. Simply enough, plants are more succulent around these water sources, and birds are attracted to that.

Huns feed early in the morning and late in the day when the weather is mild and clear. During foul or unsettled weather, Huns feed throughout the day. They glean food at a fast pace and rarely stand still for very long. Hunt likely feeding stations along the edges of crop fields, hay meadows, CRP cover, riparian draws and grasslands that have green herbs available.

After feeding, Huns will return to an open area to pick grit and loaf. Midday, during warm weather, Huns rest in the shade, under a canopy of cover such as sprawling juniper or chokecherry bushes. On hot days, Huns relax along creekbottoms, brushy draws and cool, moist areas during the midday.

Huns are about as tough as a game bird comes.

Huns also use steep hillsides to rest or relax, and occupy rock outcroppings to sun themselves in cool weather. During late fall and winter, Huns use steep sunny southern hillsides and thick cover for protection from wind and cold. During severe storms, Hungarian partridge dig holes and feed under the snow.

The brood is the core of the

Hungarian partridge can survive some awfully brutal conditions—including snow, wind and arctic cold … all at once. The birds evolved on the steppes of central Europe, enduring and even thriving under similar conditions, so it's no surprise that the birds have done well on the North American steppe.

covey, but by late fall coveys are no longer considered to be true family groups. Small groups that have lost members will combine to form a single, larger covey. Huns have adapted to industrialized farming and thrive as long as adequate nesting cover is available. If grasslands are well managed and are not overgrazed, the same is true. CRP grasslands are a boon to upland bird habitat. These large areas of renewed vegetation provide Huns good nesting habitat, roosting cover, shelter from predators and food throughout the year.

Winter weather doesn't play an important role in the gray partridges' seasonal survival. Huns are able to endure winter storms better than other introduced game birds. Adequate winter foods, suitable carry-over cover for nesting cover and other available habitat is the recipe for supporting good gray partridge populations.

Cold spring storms during and after the hatching period are believed to be responsible for losses of young birds. Chick survival also depends on the available nesting cover. Once hatched and after the critical first couple of weeks have passed, chick survival is usually good.

Hungarian partridge raise one brood a year. If a clutch is completely lost, the female will nest again but the subsequent clutch will have fewer eggs.

Hungarian partridge range.

Prairie Grasslands

As the Hun has expanded its range in North America, it has adjusted to the habitat of its ancestors—the steppes before man's intrusion—and has chosen the untilled prairie grasslands as well. Excellent gray partridge hunting exists in rolling hills, coulees, draws, bare knolls and shallow depressions running though the prairie grassland topography.

CRP Lands

In 1985 Congress enacted the Conservation Reserve Program (CRP) as the United States Department of Agriculture established a program to take marginal croplands out of production and return them to grasslands. The land enrolled in CRP calls for permanent cover—grass where grass once grew—to be allowed to rest for a period of 10 years.

Congress has since reauthorized CRP in a form similar to the previous program. Most farmers and ranchers who were in the old program stayed in the new program, and new lands were also enrolled in the revised 10-year program.

The CRP grasslands are fenced and void of livestock, which is a boon to upland bird habitat.

These large areas of renewed vegetation provide game birds with good nesting habitat, roosting cover, shelter from predators, and food, throughout the year. Huns have developed a liking for this very special habitat.

READING THE COVER

The best Hungarian partridge hunting combines the three different types of cover. These combinations come in many forms—wheatfields with many unplowed edges, rough breaks, grassy draws, or a large range of prairie grasslands with brushy draws and woody riparian habitat. Add a CRP field to the above formula and the land becomes an environmental haven for game birds. Combinations form edges and borders; some have different elevations. These are the main criteria for good Hun habitat.

Some of my favorite places to hunt for gray partridge are rolling grasslands with parallel draws and coulees. Gullies start at the ridgelines, draining down and forming draws. The draws cut deeper, creating coulees that run into the broad valleys. Most gullies have thick sage or grassy sides and sometimes rocky bottoms. Draws contain bushy vegetation and short woody plants. The coulees are wider and deeper, having steep slopes of sagebrush, juniper and grassy areas; creeks often run through them.

The cover is usually higher along a riparan draw, grassy swale or a low depression because moisture collects in low places, but partridge frequent the bottoms only at certain times of the day or season. Huns spend lots of time on grassy slopes between these low areas. For example, if two draws are one-

Simply enough, grass means Huns. It could be native grassland. But more often today it's CRP acres: set-aside, untilled land that has greatly benefited Huns (and their nesting efforts).

half mile apart, the chances of a covey in the bottom of a draw for more than a couple of hours is slim.

Look for combinations of good cover. And remember: If you hunt only agricultural land, you are missing some of the best places for Huns.

HUNTING TECHNIQUES

If the grassland is overgrazed, or the crop field is cut to the ground, forget it! The standard for any huntable Hun area is to have adequate cover.

If the birds have an excellent hatch and the coveys are numerous in the fall, hunting without a dog can be good. Without a dog, follow the edges and borders of grainfields, fencerows, patches of cover or creekbottoms where two or more cover types come together. Walk the cover where the birds should be that time of day. Scout different elevations, working the sidehills if the birds are not found in the lowlands.

Retrievers, flushing dogs and close-working pointing dogs can be very effective on Huns.

Work different elevations as you and your dogs travel through Hun country. You should stay a little higher, letting the dogs cast off from your line. Work edges, borders and seams between cover types.

Hunting with a dog, you can cover a lot of habitat thoroughly, and you'll improve your chances of finding birds. Work weedy draws, CRP fields and brushy bottomlands. Follow edges and borders where different types of cover come together.

Many hunters follow the bottom of a draw to its end and cross over to the next parallel draw, never changing elevation except for the rise and fall of the draw itself. While this method does work, you restrict yourself and the dog to only

Shotguns & Loads for Huns

Hun coveys can be approached extremely close at times. I use a 28 gauge with improved-cylinder and modified chokes. Late in the season, I recommend using a 20 gauge with improved-cylinder and full choke—not because the birds flush wild but because Huns can put a great distance between themselves and the second shot.

A fast, light gun is the answer for hunting Huns, because a lot of walking is involved and they are the fastest upland game in North America. If they are lightweight, 28, 20, 16 or 12 gauge shotguns are all adequate to use on Huns.

I start the season with No. 7½ or 8 shot in light loads. But as the season progresses and the birds mature, use No. 7½ or 6 shot in a heavier load.

one small part of the landscape. With or without a canine companion, if the country is hilly, make certain you hunt the different elevations because you'll vastly increase your chances of locating birds.

I have rangy pointing dogs, and hunt various combinations of habitat. My dogs reach out and cover a lot of ground in a short period of time. If the country I'm hunting is vast, I run more than one pointer and use beeper collars on every dog I put on the ground. Beeper collars aid greatly in locating rangy dogs on point in big country.

My preferred method is to walk the highest land forms, be it high ridges or rolling hilltops. By walking a ridge and having the dogs make long casts on both slopes and going down to the bottoms, the dogs cover all elevations, and chances of finding a covey are much greater. Not only can I observe the dogs working below me at a greater distance, but when the pointers lock up it's a lot easier walking downhill. And if the Huns flush before I arrive, I have a chance to observe the covey flying to another location.

Watch that last bird from the initial flush; it might lead you to the entire covey. Remember that individual Huns separated from the covey will hold tight after the initial flush.

After the First Flush

Once the covey is located and the shooting is over, take some mental notes. Did they hold tight? How many birds flushed? Were there any late singles? Were the birds flying low and in tight formation? Huns will often use the same maneuvers on the next flush.

Concentrate on the covey's trailing bird or any late singles that flush. The last bird will always follow the shortest route. The single, instead of going around the hill and hooking in a different direction just before landing, will take the shortest route over the top of a hill. He knows where the covey landed and will reveal their whereabouts.

After the first flush, if scenting conditions are desirable, the dogs should find the covey easily. But don't pursue the birds right after they're flushed. Let them settle in and lay down some scent. Don't follow the same course as the birds, but circle around them using the wind to your dog's advantage. If you are not successful in

Hun Sign

A gray partridge dropping is a small, circular deposit that is pale green with dark green ends. A covey usually roosts in the same area, and large circular deposits of droppings are very obvious. In warm weather, several birds sleep in a circle, but during cold nights the entire covey roosts together. Dusting bowls and relaxing areas show scattered droppings and feathers. When you find fresh droppings or roosting sites, you can be sure that birds are in the vicinity.

Hun Habits

*T*ake into account the time of year, the time of day and the weather when hunting Huns. In September, young birds feed in open areas on greens and insects. In late November, Huns feed on cereal grains such as wheat, barley and leftover oats if available, or grass and forb seeds.

If you get a Hun, take a moment to open its crop and see what the birds have been feeding on. Then hunt where the food is.

Once you have a Hun in hand, examine the crop for clues to what the birds are eating. Are they feeding on greens, insects or seeds? If you find thistle seeds, for example, look for thistle patches. It's that simple!

Birds move throughout the day and the hunter should observe daily patterns. On hot and dry days, Huns feed early morning and late afternoon. But during wet, snowy or overcast days, they will feed for long periods of time throughout the day.

Observe the cover where the first covey was flushed; they will often land in the same kind of cover. If you have previously found a roosting area by detecting several clusters of droppings, take note. When birds are pushed, they will return to a familiar site to reassemble, and roosting areas are security blankets.

Each species of game bird reacts differently on the ground when pointed by a dog. A covey of Huns will stay together as much as possible and move in the direction of their flight destination. This could be right, left, straight ahead, or the birds might hook around you. By watching your dog's movements, you can usually figure out where the birds will flush.

If you flush birds in a particular type of cover, continue your search in similar habitat.

Part of Hun country's attraction is how big and lonely it is. Crop fields, grasslands, sagebrush, hills, draws and coulees fold together to create a gorgeous backdrop for a fun hunt. You will put on some miles in your search for Huns, but sooner or later the effort will pay off.

finding the covey, begin walking a circle from where the first flush was made. If unsuccessful again, expand the circle to cover a larger radius. But as the circle gets larger, the odds of finding the covey again decrease.

The distance of a Hun's flight varies with its age. Early in September, young birds might fly only short distances and land in sight of the intruder. As the birds mature, their flight distance will increase, and usually the covey will put a hill, knoll or ridge between them and the intruder, and swing out of sight before landing. Seldom do they fly for more than a quarter mile.

Huns usually continue to fly in tight formation after being flushed more than once. When pursued, a covey will generally break up after two or three flushes and use different escape routes. Once the birds are broken up, they'll sit tight when pointed. After several flushes, the singles will often fly back to the area where they were originally flushed.

Coveys that are not hunted often hold extremely well for dogs. But like most wild game

birds, Huns get very spooky when pursued day after day. I do not pursue a single covey day after day, and I rarely work that group more than two days in a week. I have purposely worked a single covey and found that the birds become very spooky after many encounters. Coveys that have not been hunted act completely different from birds that have been harassed.

HUNTING HUNS ON THE LANDSCAPE

For years, I've hunted a large wheatfield. Along one side of the field runs an abandoned county road that leads to a rotted, weathered homestead. The outbuildings are overgrown with heavy grass, sagebrush and rows of chokecherries. Fences sag and fall on both sides of the lane.

In the center of the grainfield, a winding irrigation ditch follows the land's contours. On the other three sides of the stubble field, rolling, grassy hills climb away, but sagebrush fingers lead back down into the golden harvest.

Beyond the croplands, the rolling hill

country offers many draws filled with junipers and woody vegetation. Some have springs and creeklets. Deep gullies and ridges run parallel, leading to rocky palisades that touch the cobalt blue sky. The high grassland is managed well, and used only in the summer as pasture for cattle.

In productive years, six or seven coveys of Huns use the grainfield year-round; two live along the road. At least twenty coveys of partridge are scattered throughout the rugged, uplifted and lush grasslands. Several other coveys trade back and forth between the grassy hills and the brush ditch. This is my Hungarian partridge sanctuary.

Early in the hunting season, when the grainfield is freshly cut to stubble, the adjacent grasslands are full of insects, greens and seeds. Only the local coveys hang out around the edges of the grainfield. Later, the road and ditch coveys start using the stubble field every day.

I only hunt these coveys once or twice in the season. I return later in the hunting season when the grassland food is not as easy pickings, but the stubble field is. I have flushed 12 to 14 coveys using the stubble field.

Late one day, far out in the high-cut stubble, four pointing dogs lock up like statutes of stone. As I walk past the dogs, 28 gauge side-by-side ready, a covey of gray partridge burst from cover, flying straight into the air in tight formation. Once airborne, the swift prairie rockets level off, flying six to 10 feet above the ground at speeds of more than 40 mph, cackling a high-pitched "chrrrrrk, chrrrrrk," which sounds much like a rusty gate being opened. After hearing this sound for more than 40 years, I'm still a Hun addict.

Finding Huns

The largest distribution of Hungarian partridge is in the northwestern United States, from Lake Michigan to the Columbia River in Washington. At one time, 19 states had wild populations of gray partridge. Today, about 16 states and 3 Canadian provinces claim established populations.

North Dakota, South Dakota, Montana, Idaho, Oregon and Washington hold the highest density of gray partridge in the U.S. Alberta and Saskatchewan lead in population density in Canada. In Canada, the Huns' northern limit follows the agricultural line and stops at the edge of the boreal forest and aspen parks. Gray partridge populations in the American West occupy cropland, grassland and shrub-grasslands, but not forested areas. The area the Hun occupies today is probably the extent of the birds' usable range.

You'll find Huns—and happy Hun hunters—in grasslands and agricultural areas across the northern tier of states and southern Canada.

Working Man's Huns
By Jim Van Norman

Regardless of their "handle"—Hungarian partridge, Huns or gray partridge—these wonderful game birds are revered by the avid wing shooter as the "quail" of the high plains.

Their habitat varies here in the West, and includes stark prairies, high mountain valleys, hayfields and creekbottoms. Huns are versatile and adaptable. Seeds are their primary food requirement: weed seeds, all types of grass seeds, alfalfa seed, corn, oats, barley … you name it. They also eat bugs of all kinds. I've seen them chase grasshoppers with a vengeance.

Hunting Huns is a challenge in several ways.

First, Huns can be hard to find because of the vastness of their habitat. But if you have seen Huns in a particular area before, there is more than a good chance you will see them there again or nearby.

Second, coveys are generally spread a good distance apart and require a good bit of hiking to find, unless water is scarce. If water is in short supply, several coveys will stay reasonably close to the water source. Keep in mind though: These little birds actually require very little water and will hang around in tiny little springs that wouldn't water a crow; it may be the succulent vegetation that draws them. Preseason scouting is very helpful to find these small pockets of water throughout the hills.

Third—and I saved the best for last—when you

The country is big, the walk is long. Just when you think you've covered every nook and cranny … there they go! Try your best to get one or two now, but mark the singles carefully too; listen for their calls as they try to regroup, then go after them one by one. Huns will run a lot before the first flush, but after that—when they're alone or paired up—they'll sit much tighter.

Miles, Molly and the author (left to right) with the result of a morning's work in central Wyoming's gray partridge country.

do find Hungarian partridge they are masters at hiding and running. And they are very fast on the wing.

If Huns see you coming from a distance, they will begin running. They are very hard to catch up with. If you surprise Huns, they will hide—and hide well. They can duck down and virtually disappear, thanks to their intricate camouflage. In fact, partridge coming from alfalfa fields have a different color scheme from those that live in the prairie.

Hunt with a dog, for when you knock down several birds their coloration makes them very tough to find. All Hungarian partridge have extremely beautiful plumage when you take time to look it over.

Coveys range from half a dozen to 15 or 20 birds. A big snow tends to cause the coveys to flock together, and I've seen as many as 30 or 40 birds together after a storm. But, for the most part, 10 birds in a covey is an average.

I find a good number of birds in the hills, roosting and feeding on the south-facing slopes where the sun is warmest and grows the tallest grass and vegetation.

Once a covey is found and flushed, Hungarian partridge are very vocal. When they have landed they will call to each other to regroup. Be observant. Keep track of the calling birds so you can get into position to flush them again.

For about three hours after the sun comes up in the morning, and again from three hours before sunset, seems to be when Huns feed and move about. At midday, Huns are often shaded up under brush or rock overhangs to beat the heat; you will have to dig them out.

Very little firepower is needed to bring down a Hungarian. A short, fast-handing gun is my preference. Shotguns with skeet and improved-cylinder chokes are best. No. 7½ or 8 shot is my choice.

Chapter 12

CHUKARS: CHALLENGE IN THE ROCKS

By Ron Spomer

Chukars (far left) are colorful, handsome birds of some of the most rugged country you can imagine (left). According to the author, any number of reasons will draw you to chukar country the first time; after that, you're out for revenge.

You hunt chukars the first time for a variety of reasons: for the adventure, the challenge, the novelty, perhaps even for the dramatic scenery. After that you hunt them for revenge.

Chukars are winged demons that live on the back stoop of Hell where they laugh at mere mortals, tempting them to venture where angels fear to tread. Their siren song is hard to resist, especially when a covey perches in plain sight on a slow-roasted lava boulder above you, chuckling contemptuously. Your legs might already be burning, but somehow you'll spur yourself on.

A CHUKAR CHASE

"Let's get 'em," Joel said after we'd finally broken out of a bloody tangle of blackberry vines and tiptoed through the poison ivy patch rimming the rocky riverbank. We were in Idaho's Hell's Canyon—quintessential chukar country, and aptly named.

Although the mighty Snake River poured millions of gallons of life-giving water over the canyon floor, the broken walls hemming it in were bone dry. Native bunch grasses and invasive cheatgrass stood stiff and yellow, seldom more

Understanding Chukars

As a year progresses and changes, chukars will move (often up- or downslope) in search of the best living conditions. Water is key—in the form of standing pools or flowing streams for drinking, and in the form of a little rainfall for growing good forage.

Chukars are slightly smaller than ruffed grouse, with a stockier build and proportionately larger head. Beak to stubby tail they measure 13 to 15 inches. A mature male in prime condition will push 26 ounces, a female might hit 19 ounces.

Blue-gray plumage over crown, back, rump and stubby tail camouflages chukars nicely when they crouch among rocks and gravel to escape aerial predators. But when they stand tall to show off, they are strikingly outfitted with red bill, red eye patch, red legs, black-and-white barred flanks, white throat and black necklace that extends up and through the eyes to meet over the beak. Both sexes look alike, but mature males sport the beginnings of spurs on their legs.

Your high school English teacher would delight in informing you that the chukar's name is a classic example of international onomotopoeia, the formation of a word that sounds like the thing that makes it. In other words, the chukar's call sounds like "chukar." In Hindustani the bird is called *cakor*; in Sanskrit it's *cakora*.

Although chukars are covey birds, they break up into pairs by March, the male calling and posturing atop rocks to advertise the nesting territory and keep competitors out. By mid-September, coveys can resemble swarms, with as many as 100 birds. These coveys break up into scattered groups after autumn rains fall, but the birds coalesce again if deep snow drives them off the high slopes.

Chukars are not normally migratory, but tagged birds have been know to move nearly 40 miles over the course of a year while searching for ideal living conditions, chiefly the availability of water and forage. If you're not finding birds, don't be afraid to drive to the other side of a mountain range or into a different river system even as close as 10 miles away. You never know where highly localized conditions will have created a minor chukar population explosion.

Chukar range.

than ankle high. Just the way chukars like it.

"Shhh!" Joel held a finger up to shush me. "Hear 'em? There! See 'em hopping on the rocks? Let's go." And he started climbing, fast. "Hurry! We're almost in range."

An hour later we dragged ourselves over the rim of a dry finger ridge, gasping, sweating, parched. But we figured we had the birds cornered. We'd seen them scoot over the top, and now that we were there we could see there was no more "up" for them to run. We checked our chambers, lifted our double-barrels to port arms and began kicking clumps of bunchgrass along the broken rimrock edge.

Chukar country is invariably steep, dry or rugged … and usually all three. Be ready for the challenge, because this bird is tougher to hunt than almost any other. Knowing chukars, and how they use their habitat, will help you find birds.

The covey flushed with a wonderful roar, practically at our feet. But instead of flying up, those contrary birds flew down—dived, really—every one of them ducking beneath our shot swarms, leaving us fuming in the heat. We counted 28 birds gliding across the big side canyon before they landed on the far side—near the bottom.

A half hour later—gasping, sweaty, parched— we too reached the canyon floor. Of course the birds were no longer there, having started up the far side without us. But we heard them chuckling at their little joke.

This is the standard chukar escape drill. Run up, fly down, run up again and leave terrestrial predators in the dust. When hard pressed, the birds hide among broken outcroppings and boulders that further slow attackers, even hawks. Joel's eyes flashed vengeance. "Didja hear that? They can't be more than a hundred yards above us …"

For some hunters, just one of these predatory adventures is enough. But, like chronic gamblers, the weak-willed get hooked. They know the odds are stacked against them, but they keep coming back. Just one more try. This could be the big one, the day we corner the covey, shoot like Annie Oakley and erase all the losses.

Actually, chukar hunting isn't as impossible as we hyperbolic writers make it sound. True, much of the best chukar habitat is frighteningly steep, dry and rugged, but some is merely steep, dry and rocky. Experienced hunters athletically work with good dogs to regularly bag four to eight birds a day. The trick is knowing chukars, chukar habitat and how the birds relate to it.

THE KEYS TO THE KINGDOM

Native to the dry foothills of the Himalayas, chukars reached American shores only when sportsmen gave them a free ride over and turned them loose. Despite dozens of stockings coast to coast throughout the first half of the 20th century, the partridges "took" only in Western habitat that closely matched their original homeland—dry, steep and rocky grassland sprinkled with small shrubs and running streams or perennial springs.

You can see all the components of good chukar country in this scene: steep, vertical terrain; rocks, bluffs and cuts; cheatgrass; and a little water. Chukar heaven!

CRITICAL HABITAT COMPONENTS

When shopping for real estate in which to raise a family, chukars insist on four ingredients. If any are missing, so are the birds.

• **Vertical terrain.** Not cliffs, but not gentle grades either. We're talking significant angles here—the kind that make you pause before starting up, and rest often once you do. Let's call it 25 degrees and steeper on average. There will be exceptions, but this is a good rule of thumb.

• **Exposed rocks.** These can be rimrock, rocky outcroppings or scattered boulders. They may be more or less continuous over the landscape or sprinkled here and there. There's no hard-and-fast rule on just how much of this exposed rock chukars require, but there has to be some. Steep, nearly vertical badlands bluffs, cuts and erosion channels are an acceptable substitute in some areas.

• **Cheatgrass.** This is an annual grass native to the chukar's original Asian home. It came to the U.S. in wheat seed imported from the old country. This short-stemmed grass produces lots of seeds that sprout with the first autumn rains. Cold and snow might shut down photosynthesis, but the first warm spell fires it up again. By the time native grasses begin their spring growth, cheatgrass has "cheated" them out of much early-season moisture and fertility. It quickly sets seed and dies. Green cheat provides vitamin-rich forage in fall and winter. The seeds provide carbohydrate energy during periods of drought.

• **Water.** In most chukar habitat this is usually a creek or river, the birds coming down daily to drink, but many times mountain springs high up the slopes provide this essential element. During spring and autumn rains, small pools enable birds to spread far and wide.

Make sure these four ingredients are present, to give yourself a fighting chance of finding a chukar in the country you're going to hunt.

Shotguns & Loads for Chukars

A chukar gun is not a showpiece—unless you want to show the dent in the barrel where you wrapped it around a rock, the chip in the stock where it broke your fall or the long scratches where it tobogganed down a slope.

Think military—something that will take a licking and keep on shooting. Light is good unless you have a gun bearer. Quick helps, but long range potential is also useful. So is firepower. The gentlemanly double barrel is fine for pheasants or quail, and usually for chukars. But when you finally catch up to the covey that's been giving you the slip all day, you might want to extract your pound of flesh. Quite often your best chance comes after you've hastily blown your second shot. That's when one or two late birds will flush at your feet. On these occasions a pump or autoloader is worth its weight in water, which is itself worth more than gold near the end of a hot September hunt.

But choose a gun you shoot well regardless of action style or gauge. Some shooters score better with 28 gauge doubles than 12 gauge autos simply because the smaller gun is easier to carry all day, quicker to swing into action and more natural to point.

All else being equal, a 12 bore will give you a few extra yards over all others. I've found a 6-pound, over-and-under 20 gauge with 28-inch tubes nearly the perfect compromise, but I'm about to switch to a 6-pound Beretta AL391 auto 20 gauge, plain Jane version, that fits me like a glove.

Choke requirements vary day to day, but improved cylinder is hard to beat with modified the second most useful. On early hunts cylinder or skeet chokes aren't too open, and full choke is useful on some late hunts. Go with interchangeable tubes if possible and change as required.

Chukars are tough, but they're not pheasants. Stick with light charges of No. 7½ shot in all gauges early, switching to 6 shot when they begin flushing farther out. But pattern first. Most 28s and some 20s pattern 6s poorly. Better a dense, even pattern of 7½s. The 12 will handle 5 and 4 shot, but those are rarely required, the latter leaving chukar-sized holes in most patterns at the extreme ranges where their retained energy is needed. Buffered loads of copper-plated shot can help keep things together for those long shots.

Don't take your fancy shotgun chukar hunting; the rocks and the adventure will punish it badly. That said, do carry a light gun (most any gauge will do), choked improved-cylinder early in the season, modified or even full later on. No. 7½ shot is good for most chukar days.

LOOK & LISTEN

Once you find the four conditions (page 120), you're ready to find chukars, and not just by stomping the slopes. A saner approach is to look and listen. Chukars are notoriously noisy, especially early and late in the day.

Sit quietly for 10 minutes with your ears pricked for chukars' distinctive cackling calls that sound as if the birds are repeating their name. Sort of "chukar chukar chukar chuka ka ka ka kak," sometimes "kakada kakada kakada," harsh and rather high pitched.

Beware of the echoes so common in canyons. You don't want to hike even 300 feet up a slope only to hear distinctly on the opposite slope the birds you first thought you heard on your slope. It's a confusing game. It helps if two or more hunters listen 50 or 100 yards apart in order to triangulate the sound.

If your quarry is silent, initiate the conversation with a few rudimentary cackles of your own. You'll catch on once you hear a real bird, but don't be shy about scratching out any kind of "cack cack cacking" with your own voice. Chukars are either quite accepting of poor quality calls or nearly tone deaf, because I've heard them talk back to the sorriest facsimile of a chukar call ever to escape a human larynx. The important thing is to get some cackling noise bouncing around the hills.

Should your attempts at conversation be rebuffed, grab a pair of binoculars and scan the rocks. Except when midday sun drives them to shade, your quarry delights in perching atop boulders to watch for predators. Until midmorning, coveys feed actively across sparsely vegetated slopes, picking various leaves and seeds, and catching grasshoppers and other insects.

Barring confirmation of game with your ears or eyes, you play the odds. And those vary by season, habitat, time of day and weather.

CHUKAR DOGS

Any well-trained dog can help a great deal on a chukar hunt. Retrievers are lifesavers for bringing back birds that fall hundreds of yards out. Pointers are real work savers when they cast high and low to search ground you haven't the time or energy to work. Chukars usually hold well for points, but in very broken terrain it's a challenge to keep old Rover in sight. Try a locator collar. White dogs show up better than dark and also handle the heat better—until it snows, when dark dogs gain the advantage.

Introduce a new dog gradually to cliff habitat. More than one exuberant mutt has run off a cliff to its death. To prevent this, walk your dog on a lead to several cliffs, short and tall. Show him the precipices. Take him up and down a few tough

A good dog can really help you on a chukar hunt—both in the finding and retrieving of birds.

spots, narrow canyons, rock chimneys and the like. Then hunt him close and slowly if possible until he shows enough sense to run cliff country cautiously. Most dogs catch on quickly.

While you're at it, snake-proof your four-legged partner. Rattlesnakes are common in much good chukar country, so why take chances? To snake-proof, set the dog up with a de-fanged rattler or any harmless snake. Put an electronic collar on the dog, then walk it on a leash toward the snake in plain view. When the dog moves in close, zap it. Don't say anything, don't comfort it. Just lead it away.

Next, hide the snake so the dog can only smell it. When the dog shows interest in the snake scent, zap it. Finally, set up a hidden tape player with a recorded snake rattle or rig an actual snake rattle on a stick and have someone shake it. When the dog shows interest and moves in, zap it. Check the dog's response at the start of each season. If it seems to have forgotten the lessons, repeat them.

When the sun is hot, chukars seek shade of any kind, like the brush in the background here.

EARLY-SEASON HUNTING

Water is the key when most chukar seasons open in September, and summer's drought has reduced options to running streams or perennial springs. This is good for hunters because it limits the birds' range, forcing them off the high slopes and ridges. In fact, one of the most popular hunting tactics is to boat rivers, looking and listening for birds. Beach, circle above them and have at it. Disturbed coveys may run surprisingly far upslope, but by late afternoon they're usually back, so you don't have to kill yourself climbing in the heat. Just work near water, looking and listening before you strike. Always approach from above or the birds will tow you uphill.

Streams too shallow to float can be walked. Stay slightly above the banks to avoid riparian brush, although you'll usually find bonus valley quail there. Chukars will loaf in surprisingly dense brush to escape the hot sun.

Springs can be tough to find because they often seep from the bottoms of narrow side canyons. Look for oases of green on dried-up slopes. These can be small as a 10-foot circle of brush or a long, skinny line of willows dribbling down a slope. Sometimes watering holes aren't green at all, but bare, dark and muddy from cattle stomping them. Finding any isolated watering hole can be a bonanza, the daily meeting point for every chukar for thousands of yards around.

The downside to the early season is heat. It's difficult to carry enough water for you and your dogs, so hunt early and late (saving midday for siesta and a swim) or hunt shady brush near water. Dust and heat also ruin scenting conditions, another reason to hunt early mornings.

If you can't target water sources in the early season, at least leave a drop-off vehicle on a high ridge and zigzag down toward another vehicle where you've stashed plenty of water. If you're limited to one truck, park it low and hunt up first. It's easier to hike down than up at the end of a long, hot day. Aim for grassy foraging slopes and flats early, steep and rocky escape cover later or after birds have been disturbed, and shady brush once the sun grows fierce.

This period begins after the first fall rains, which change everything. As water pools, chukars spread out and move back upslope, especially if cheatgrass also sprouts. After a dry summer they're hungry for fresh salad. Now you'll really have to cover country to find them. Listening and looking are your best bets. Green cheatgrass patches are worth hiking to if they're few and far between.

The good news is that your dog should be able to scent better in the moist air; depend on him to vacuum the slopes. And hunt sidehill and downhill as much as possible to conserve your energy. The standard two-vehicle drop-off saves time and energy. If you find birds, hunt at that level to find more. Also note the habitat where they were foraging or loafing, and look for similar stuff.

Try to discover a pattern. Watch for tracks in mud around puddles, black-and-white droppings anywhere. Because chukars almost always fly level

The search for chukars will take you to many rugged places.

or down, stagger your team vertically up and down any slope, then work it horizontally as much as possible, staying abreast or nearly so. Lower hunters almost always get shots at plunging birds bumped from above.

Boots & Vests

An army marches on its stomach, a hunter marches in his boots, and nowhere are sturdy boots more important. You want stiff lug soles with hard, sharp edges that you'll use to cut into sidehills, literally standing on edge. The stiff sole keeps your foot from rolling down. (It's like standing on skis stuck into a vertical wall.) The lugs grip small projections of rocks and help you negotiate ledges.

The hardest rubber outsoles will last longest, but slightly softer rubber will grip wet surfaces better. Tall uppers, 8 to 10 inches and with a bit of padding, protect ankles against twisting and being poked by sharp rocks. Good uppers keep

You need good boots and a properly stocked vest to tackle chukar country.

stones and debris out. Beware of big hook eyelets. They can catch opposite lace loops or pants cuffs and send you face first down a hill. Not fun. Tie laces off short and secure them with a wrap of duct tape for safety.

You'll need a lot of room in your vest for shells, lunch, first aid kit for man and beast, lots of water and, of course, birds. Take a heavy zip-top bag for your dog's drinking bowl. Two liters of water are good for half a day in early season. Some vests include flexible bladders that fit against your back and are drained through a hose. You'll work up a hunger after a few hours and so will your pooch. Carry a quick energy treat for him as well as yourself.

124

LATE-SEASON HUNTING

This hunting period usually starts with snow. Chukars don't like it, so it forces them low. A favorite tactic of chukar pros is to hunt just at or under the snowline. Sometimes a canyon's entire partridge population will be squeezed within a narrow belt of snow-free ground near the bottom of a canyon. It doesn't get any easier than that.

Winter coveys also join into big, noisy flocks. Glassing and listening still work beautifully. You often find your quarry's tracks in the snow and sometimes you can follow them right to their makers.

When snow covers everything right down to the creeks and temperatures plummet, hunt the south slopes. Snow is usually shallowest there due to sun melt, and south slopes always open first. On cold, clear mornings, glass the bases of dark cliffs, boulders or clumps of sage for huddled birds soaking up some sun.

THE CHUKAR CHALLENGE

Chukars make for some maddening hunting, to be sure: a blend of climbing, hiking, scrambling and shooting across some of the earth's most hellaciously steep and rocky country. But the challenge and allure—both of the bird and of his desolately wild home—will keep you coming back for more.

Finding Chukars

Chukars live in several Western states, but the Big Four are southwest Idaho, eastern Oregon, northern Nevada and northern Utah. Southeast and central Washington can build good concentrations in the channeled scablands, Okanogan valley and Snake and Columbia River breaks after dry nesting seasons. Wyoming boasts a few hot spots from the southwest up through the center of the state. In Montana chukars are rare outside of southern Carbon County east of Red Lodge and west of the Pryor Mountains. California's birds are in the northeast and parts of the east-central desert mountains. Look in the dry northwest corner of Colorado. Grand Junction is a good starting point. For a real adventure, check out the semi-deserts and lava rock grasslands on Hawaii!

Annual chukar populations vary greatly from state to state and region to region within those states. Always contact the appropriate state wildlife agency for up-to-date information before launching a trip.

A couple conversations with game agency biologists can steer you to places with chukars.

Chapter 13

Spring Turkeys: Calling Magnificent Gobblers

By Bill Hollister

Wild turkeys are our most widespread upland game bird, with a spring hunting season open in 49 states! Whether you hunt them in the North, South, East or West, you're after one of the most alert, wary, beautiful and majestic birds alive (far left). And even when he's not in an especially suspicious mood, a gobbler sneaks along as a matter of everyday business anyway (left).

*I*n the inky blackness of a cool spring morning, I paused on an oak ridge just to listen. A whip-poorwill sounded off in the distance. Then a barred owl chimed in, followed by another. I walked a short distance, pausing again in time to hear the melodious song of a male cardinal.

The eastern sky was beginning to lighten with hues of pink and blue, but the sound I longed to hear—the gobble of a wild turkey—didn't materialize. A short distance farther, I met an old hunter who said that earlier, in the darkness, he had flushed what he thought were two turkeys from

their roost. He decided to set up where he was. I headed off in the direction the turkeys had flown.

Several hundred yards later I stopped again and stroked a few very unsure yelps on my Lynch box call. To my astonishment, two birds gobbled back. Minutes later I made three rather feeble yelps on the box, and before I had finished the third note, gobbles broke into my call. The birds were closer!

I hunkered down behind a large beech log and waited, my heart beating like a triphammer. Soon two turkeys strolled slowly into the clearing in front of me. The lead bird, smaller with a short

127

beard, kept on a steady pace. A big gobbler occasionally fanned its huge tail and seemed reluctant to close the distance to me. When the larger tom stepped from behind a big hemlock some 30 yards away, I centered the bead on his head and fired. He folded momentarily, then went airborne behind the hemlock and disappeared into the valley below. I concluded that shooting an old open-choked Browning Auto 5 that had been fine on ruffed grouse and ringnecks just didn't cut it when it came to killing these big birds.

In retrospect, I should have taken the much closer jake. I spent most of the morning looking for the bird I'd shot at, to no avail. I vowed right there that I would be better armed and would not make the same mistakes again.

This happened more than three decades ago, but it got me hooked. I have continued my quest for this king of game birds every spring and fall since.

Step one to a classic hunt: Know where a gobbler is roosted. Then you're not "hunting blind" the next morning.

SCOUTING

Preseason scouting is important if you will be hunting on your own. Cruise back roads at dusk and especially at dawn. Stop every half mile. Listen intently, and use locator calls to try to elicit a response from a roosted gobbler. You just want to know they are there; you do not want to call them in.

More important, walk ridges at dawn and dusk for a few weeks leading up to the spring season opener, trying to locate birds "back in." These birds, roosted away from roads in secluded hollows or remote areas, generally have not been "talked to" much before season. You might have them all to yourself on opening day and that, of course, would be a real plus.

While walking ridges and valleys before the season starts, look for turkey scratchings and dusting areas where turkeys wallow and dust to rid themselves of bird lice. Look for feathers, droppings, tracks and any other clues that indicate turkeys are using the area. In early morning, listen for hens

These gobblers are in "strut" position: tail feathers spread, body feathers erect and heads pulled in. Chances are they're "drumming" too. This is a sight turkey hunters live for! But just as often, you'll see a bird approaching in his normal "slicked" plumage, or sneaking in suspiciously (previous pages).

128

sounding off with soft tree calls while on roost, fly-down cackles or yelping. Of course, always try to tune in to the gobbling of toms that may be heard for nearly a mile on a still spring morning. Also, listen for wingbeats as birds fly down from roosts at dawn or fly up to roost at dusk.

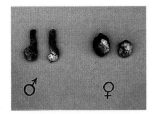

Gobbler droppings (left) are J- or hook-shaped; hen droppings (right) are simple blobs. Knowing the difference helps to discern whether you've located a concentration of gobblers or hens.

SETTING UP

Setting up is just one aspect—albeit an important one—of a successful hunt. If the foliage isn't leafed out and if you know where a gobbler is roosted, try to set up 125 to 150 yards from him, in darkness, at least on the same level as he is but preferably above him. Later in the season, with full foliage, try to set up before light about 75 yards from his roost tree.

Avoid physical barriers that may present obstacles to the gobbler as he approaches your call site. High woven-wire fences, deep ravines, wide expanses of water and even thick brush may discourage a gobbler from closing the distance to you.

Setting up on roosted birds at dawn is one thing. But should you get an initial response from a gobbler that is on the ground at any time of day, try to estimate the distance between you and him. If cover and contours permit, close the distance. Remember: A real hen will have a tendency to move toward the tom, and you should do the same. Stop periodically when closing the distance and call again; if the gobbler answers, you might be able to tell if he is coming in. If so, don't push it. Get set up now and be ready!

If at all possible, choose a tree wider than your shoulders both to break up your outline and to provide you with some safety should another hunter approach you from the rear.

If the tree you choose is one that stands alone with a clearing all around, you might stick out like the proverbial "sore thumb." In this case you might better choose a tree set back from the clearing where you will blend in better.

A decoy or two set up 20 or 25 yards in front of you is often just what "old tom" will be looking for. If you don't use decoys, try to ensure that when the gobbler first steps into view, he will be within range or close to it. Always be ready to make your shot. Being "ready" means (1) pointing your left shoulder in the direction you last heard the gobbler if you shoot right-handed and (2) having your shotgun in a position where minimal movement is required to be on target and you can easily "cheek-down" on the stock.

Here's a classic and safe setup: The hunter's back is against a tree wider than his shoulders. It's also classic in that the turkey is coming in from the direction least expected!

Understanding the Wild Turkey

As spring develops in the countryside, toms gobble mightily to advertise their services to any listening hens. The birds also fight feverishly to establish a pecking order that will define which bird dominates the others for breeding rights.

No matter what the subspecies, wild turkey behavior is similar.

During the winter months, turkeys generally flock up in separate groups consisting of: hens with their female young; old gobblers; and jakes. But as daylight hours lengthen in late winter and early spring, the pituitary glands trigger hormones in both gobblers and hens to begin the breeding cycle. In the North, much interaction between gobblers and hens occurs during March, April and into May when most spring hunting seasons are ongoing. In the Deep South this activity occurs as much as five to seven weeks earlier, and in southern Florida some hunting seasons open as early as the first week in March.

As gobblers separate from their winter flocks, toms do a lot of strutting, following hens around and beginning to establish a hierarchy. Now a dominant tom will often tolerate other toms around him as he accumulates a harem of hens. Dominant toms do a lot of posturing and not a lot of gobbling during this period. Prior to the breeding season, gobblers have built up a large quantity of stored fat called "breast sponge" that will sustain them during this period when they do a lot of breeding and very little feeding.

The actual breeding period may occur over a period of more than two months. In the Northeast I've observed breeding as early as April 11 and as late as May 26. During this breeding phase, gobbling activity usually increases dramatically—especially at dawn when gobblers are gathering hens. As turkey seasons open, hunters afield often remark that gobblers seem to shut down shortly after coming off roost. This is common, as dominant toms have hens all around them and are occupied with showing off and mating for a considerable period after leaving their nightly roosts.

Later in the season, when hens leave the dominant toms to begin the 26- to 28-day incubation period, another phase occurs. Hens will leave the nest for only short periods to feed, and will generally avoid any contact with gobblers. Toms still interested in mating begin to see hens leaving them. Gobbling activity often increases and, from my experience, this is the time to bag your all-time trophy gobbler.

There are no hard-and-fast calendar dates when different phases of spring breeding activity occurs. Although photoperiod or amount of daylight hours triggers breeding activity, weather, latitude and

Wild turkey nest and eggs.

other factors can have a bearing. For instance, an early spring often creates the best hunting during the early part of the season, with noticeably diminished activity late in the season. But during a late spring, hunting is often better during the latter part of the season.

Also keep in mind that gobbling response often increases when clearing occurs after a sudden shower or thunderstorm. The same is true after prolonged bad weather. When the front moves out and sunshine returns can be a dynamite time to be afield.

Following the breeding season, yet another phase occurs. Toms, true male chauvinists, gather again in even-aged groups, while hens take on total responsibility in raising their young.

= Eastern
= Merriam's
= Gould's
= Rio Grande
= Osceola (Florida)

Survivors run.

THE GRAND SPRING HUNT

I left my truck well before dawn and picked my way up a long logging road leading to a hardwood ridge. The smells and sounds of the spring woods were all around me. It was great to be alive and to witness daybreak from my ridgetop. I heard no turkey sounds during the early hours, so I ventured to another spot about a mile away. Here I walked slowly up a logging road toward a horse pasture, where a few days before I had seen two gobblers strutting.

Standing in the roadway, I sounded some soft yelps on my box call. Gobbles erupted from what I thought were two birds less than 100 yards away. I scrambled to get set up against the nearest tree and to get my face mask in place. No sooner did I get my shotgun across my knee when the two gobblers appeared, both strutting majestically toward me. Rain the night before left water droplets glimmering like diamonds on the early spring foliage, and the copper and bronze of the gobblers' breast feathers shone iridescent in the dappled sunlight.

At 30 yards both birds gobbled. I'm sure the hair on my neck was standing straight out; I thought my heart would burst. I regained my composure just enough to center the bead on the neck of the closest bird and squeeze the trigger. The whole matter was over in minutes and I'm sure it took only seconds to reach my first spring gobbler.

Not one but two gobblers approached the author. He took that first bird many years (and more than a hundred turkeys) ago.

131

To say I was overwhelmed would be an understatement. I marveled at the beauty of the feathers and the size of the bird's body, beard and spurs. I savored the moment and, while my encounters with these great game birds number in the hundreds now, I still experience those same emotions today. Each gobbler worked provides treasured memories of battles won and lost.

HUNTING THE EARLY SEASON

Opening day of the spring turkey season is looked upon with great anticipation, though it may not differ greatly from many other days of the season depending on the mood of your quarry. This classic and time-honored strategy is still the best one: put a bird to bed. That is, go out the evening before and locate a roosted gobbler that you will have all to yourself the next morning.

I've done this many times in preparation for opening morning, but one classic hunt comes to mind. I had owl-hooted a bird that responded well at dusk. He was roosted about 100 yards above a logging road in an area I knew intimately. Well before dawn, I was in position, seated against a large oak approximately 125 yards uphill from where the tom had been the evening before.

My first owl-hoot brought a response, but the gobbler was above me! Convinced that the bird I'd heard the night before was still roosted below me, I stayed put. About 20 minutes before fly-down time, I sounded the soft notes of a tree call. Again only the bird roosted above me gobbled. The next 10 minutes were fraught with indecision; should I stay put or try to get above or at least try to reach the same contour level of the bird that was responding? Thinking it was too risky, I stayed put.

Lying next to me was a hen turkey wing that I had dried and braced with aluminum that was covered with camo tape. I'd carried this with me for nearly 20 years and at times it had worked wonders. Just prior to fly-down time, I made two sequences of fly-down cackles accompanied by beating the wing against my leg. To my surprise, five gobblers literally shook the trees! One was above me, while four were roosted below.

The next half hour was action packed. The bird roosted above me flew down first, followed by the four below me. In a matter of minutes that seemed like an hour, a jake and two longbeards cautiously approached my call site. A sharp putt brought one longbeard out of strut just as my load of number 5s connected, to end a classic but short opening day hunt.

Natural sounds such as those made by my hen wing—as well as scratching in the leaves to get a reluctant tom to close the distance to you—can make for a successful hunt at any time.

Most early-season hunting finds juvenile toms (jakes) and satellite toms (usually two-year-old birds) responsive, while dominant older gobblers are often henned-up and reluctant to come to your calls.

Early season has its challenges: The gobblers are still ganged up and are often very shy of coming in as a whole group. Plus, a lack of foliage makes it harder for a hunter to hide.

On one opening day hunt, I spotted five jakes in an open field. Jakes or adult gobblers with hens in this situation can be extremely difficult to call in. Knowing that jakes like to watch a fight, I crawled up behind a large birch log and began a lengthy sequence of challenge or fighting purrs on a diaphragm call. At the same time, I began beating my hen wing on the log in front of me. The five jakes, which were more than 100 yards away, began racing toward me to see who could get there first. With only my eyes, camo cap and gun barrel showing above the log, I continued to beat the wing against the log even when the birds were less than 15 yards from me. Their reaction was to walk back and forth purring and putting and acting puzzled at what was going on. They were in no rush to leave the scene. I passed on the jakes, but this experience alone made for an interesting opening day.

Turkey Hunting Safety

Hunting, in general, is a very safe outdoor pursuit. But turkey hunting by its very nature provides elements that differ dramatically from other types of hunting: hunters are camouflaged, the hunt is up close and personal, you're vocalizing the quarry's calls … all are reasons to make safety paramount.

Some hunters, seeing that friends and acquaintances have filled their tags, look upon their quest to kill a gobbler as a competitive situation. But remember that the only competition is between you and the turkey; there should be no reason for desperation, a cause of many accidents.

Turkey hunting safety is crucial at the setup point, but don't forget hunting's basic safety rules at other stages of the hunt either.

A simple step toward avoiding accidents is to be aware of what is going on around you and to follow basic common sense. Treat your shotgun as if it were loaded by ensuring that it is always pointed in a safe direction. Make sure it is unloaded when it's not in use, and be sure of your target and beyond.

Never stalk a bird … you might be approaching a calling hunter. Rather, set up and call birds to you. Sit against a tree or other object that is wider than your shoulders; this will protect you from the rear and give you the opportunity to see anyone approaching from the front or sides. If another hunter walks into view, signal him in a clear and loud voice. Do not wave, whistle or make any sounds that could be mistaken for a turkey call!

Wear camouflage clothing and do not wear anything that has red, white or blue—all turkey colors.

Don't compete with another hunter already working a bird. Instead be safe and ethical; walk away and find another gobbler to work, or come back another day.

Remember, no turkey in the world is worth putting yourself or a fellow hunter in a position where an accident could occur. This is every turkey hunter's responsibility!

MID-SEASON HUNTING

Most turkey hunters with a number of spring seasons under their belt have experienced periods when it appears every gobbler around has a bad case of "lockjaw." This often occurs with hunting pressure and after a number of the most vulnerable birds—jakes and two-year-old toms—have been taken. Dominant gobblers, still with hens, are reluctant to "talk" much after coming off roost.

These older, henned-up toms present a real challenge. They can often be observed strutting in open fields with their hens.

Mid-season has its challenges: The gobblers, sticking close to the now-friendly hens, often don't have much reason to check out your calls. Why go to an unseen teaser in the brush when there are lovely and willing hens right at your side?

Sometimes cutting and excited calling to the hens will prompt a response from the boss hen and she

Hunting with a Partner

Spring turkey hunting is often a one-on-one situation between you and your quarry, but hunting with a partner certainly has benefits. Two minds are often better than one in developing a strategy. And a caller, set up 20 to 30 yards behind the shooter, can often lure a bird into that 60-yard "hang-up" range ... which puts him 30 yards from the shooter! Plus reluctant toms, especially late in the season, often hang back even farther, giving the caller an opportunity to retreat and call like a departing hen; sometimes this will cause an old tom to break and come close enough for a lethal shot.

Turkey hunting with a partner can sometimes be more productive than going it alone.

Despite these advantages, I still find it most successful when sitting right next to your hunting partner, usually against the same big tree. Whether your hunting partner is a newcomer or an "old hand" at this game, the ability to communicate (by whispers) as a gobbler gets in close often makes the difference between going home with a trophy gobbler over your shoulder or just a pleasant memory of another day in the turkey woods.

will come and investigate with the other hens and the gobbler following. But this is rare at best.

Observe where the birds exit the field or better yet, if you see them coming into a field, note the time and make sure you get there before they do the following day.

But my best strategy on hunting henned-up gobblers who have been coming to large open fields to strut is to arrive before daylight. Set up where you have seen them come in or leave the area. You might want to construct a makeshift blind. Place your decoys—a couple of hens and a jake—within 20 or 25 yards of your setup. Call sparingly with soft yelps and clucks, and be extremely patient. The waiting may be akin to long hours spent on a deer stand, but this method is very effective when gobblers are not talking and appear to be henned-up.

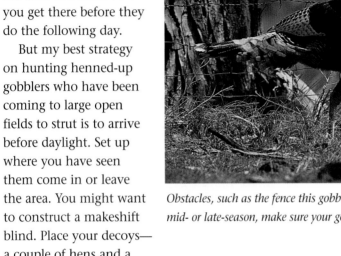

Obstacles, such as the fence this gobbler is approaching, are your enemy at any setup. Early-, mid- or late-season, make sure your gobbler has a clear and easy path to you.

LATE-SEASON HUNTING

No matter what part of the country you're in, late in the spring turkey season can be the least pleasant to be afield. But it can also be the most rewarding. Hot weather, as well as too many nights with little sleep, take their toll on our human frailties. Mosquitoes, black flies, ticks, chiggers and other pests can frustrate even the most dedicated turkey hunters. But with full foliage on, you can now slip within 75 or 80 yards of a roosted gobbler. These longbeards now have few or sometimes no hens with them.

Being in close will give you the edge in getting that tom to come to you right off the roost before any remaining hens get to him. If you are set up close, a barely audible tree call might be all you need just to let him know you are there. A soft fly-down with a wing or flapper just before first light could bring him to your lap.

In the late season, I often do not call until I hear the gobbler fly down. These dominant toms that have had hens with them for weeks are no dummies. They have been used to having hens come to them, and too much calling while the gobbler is on roost will keep him up there.

When a gobbler does fly down, he might just walk away from you. If you

The author, shown here, believes late-season hunting can be the best hunting.

Shotguns & Loads for Wild Turkey

The most popular turkey gun by far is the 12 gauge. After my first experience with not killing a turkey with an open-choked 12 gauge, the following spring season found me afield with a Browning Auto 5, 3-inch magnum 12 gauge. It did the job well that second year and has performed superbly over the subsequent three decades on both spring and fall birds.

I purchased the Browning equipped with a 30-inch full-choke barrel when long barrels were the rage for turkey guns. I've since replaced the "long tom" barrel with a 24-inch Hastings barrel with internal choke tubes and while I have a number of chokes including an extra-full, I still rely on the regular full choke when hunting both spring and fall gobblers. Most turkey hunting experts agree that barrel lengths of 24 or 26 inches are ideal. Longer barrels make it difficult to swing past saplings and brush for a shot.

I've patterned my Browning Auto 5 and my Winchester 1300 12 gauge 3-inch magnums with all types of turkey loads and chokes until my right shoulder was black and blue. I've shot Federal, Remington, Winchester, Fiocchi and others in a variety of shot sizes and have killed turkeys with shot sizes ranging from 2s to 7½s. The one load that patterns best for me and has been most effective afield is the Winchester Supreme with 1¾ ounces of No. 5 shot in a 3-inch magnum shell.

Armed with the right shotgun and teamed up with the right friends, anyone can kill a turkey stone-cold.

Many turkey hunters have gone to the 12 gauge 3½-magnum which appears to be increasingly popular. Some hunters even go with the 10 gauge. While both may increase effective range, they are certainly not as comfortable to shoot as the 3-inch magnum 12, and patterning them off a bench rest with multiple shots can be a very unpleasant experience.

I have a Tru-glo fiber-optic sight on one turkey gun and a Hi Viz on the other. Both are wonderful aids when shooting at a turkey, especially in poor light conditions. Many hunters have gone to the Aimpoint or other low-power scopes on their turkey guns and they do help to pinpoint your shot. Unlike most shotgun shooting where you point-and-shoot, when turkey hunting you must aim your shotgun as you would a rifle.

Short of having one of these sights on your gun, a second bead—midway down the rib—is important for making sure you get your cheek down on the stock and don't shoot over the bird. Just line up both beads before taking a shot!

The obvious advantages of using a scope include the ability to adjust windage and elevation to ensure that your shot pattern is properly centered on your target, and the opportunity to see your entire target rather than blocking most of it out by your barrel. When my eyesight gets worse or I get so old that I start missing, I might have to switch to a scope.

are unsuccessful at first light, try again later in the morning, especially in areas where you might have seen him strutting with hens.

In nature, the tom gobbles and the hens go to him. To reverse nature and get the tom to come to you often requires more than just good calling. Proper setup, sound strategy, skilled woodsmanship, proficient calling and above all, patience and persistence, are the hallmarks of any successful turkey hunter. Late season can be the most rewarding time to put all this knowledge to work. It is the period when you are most likely dealing with dominant toms. And it also provides you with the greatest challenges, and the opportunity to go home with your all-time best trophy limb-hanger.

TURKEY CALLS

The wild turkey's vocabulary is extensive and, while you need not know every sound a turkey makes, you should know the basics of those used most commonly in springtime: the yelp, cutt, cluck, purr and gobble. A good tape or CD can give you these sounds to practice to.

Most experienced spring turkey hunters share the opinion that it is necessary to become reasonably proficient with both air-operated and friction calls. To a turkey *hunter's* ear, nothing sounds better than a diaphragm call in the mouth of an expert. I've had the pleasure to judge major calling competitions in six states and at two U.S. Opens, and I can vouch for the fact that these competition callers seldom make a mistake, but turkeys sometimes sound like they do. To the *turkey's* ear, I'm convinced that nothing sounds better than a rather high-pitched, raspy old friction call, especially a box call. This is particularly true later in the spring season when birds have listened to about every type of diaphragm call imaginable.

Box calls, push-pin calls, peg-and-slate and

The author believes that a raspy old box call rings most true to a cagey old gobbler's ears.

Peg-and-slate calls make great turkey calls, although it can take a bit of practice to master making the proper motions to get good turkey sounds.

Blow a locator call to get a turkey to gobble and reveal his whereabouts. Locating a gobbler with turkey sounds might bring him running before you're set up and ready.

others that use friction to make the sound are relatively easy to master. Three of my favorites are HS Strut's Li'l Deuce, Knight and Hale's Ol' Yeller and Scotch's Glass Over Slate. As stated, a fine way to learn yelps, cutts, clucks and purrs is by listening to tapes and mimicking the sounds you hear. Better still, record some of your own calls on a cassette recorder and play them back to see how realistic your own calls sound. Calls made by real hen turkeys, either recorded or by spending enough time in the woods to hear them first hand, can be a tremendous learning experience.

Air-operated calls are generally more difficult to master, especially the diaphragm and wing-bone-type calls. The key to using a diaphragm call is to ensure a tight seal between the roof of your mouth and the call and to make sure that all air expelled from deep in your chest and throat is passed between your tongue and the call.

Diaphragms leave both hands free when you are making your shot: a real advantage. For long distance calling, the wingbone is particularly effective. Both box calls and air-operated shaker-type or bellows calls can make the gobble, a call I seldom use in the spring turkey woods for safety reasons.

Locator calls on the market today are almost too numerous to mention. Locator calls do just that—locate a gobbler by making him "shock gobble" without the risk of calling him in to you before you're ready. This is the first step that initiates your strategy of where to set up.

Most hunters do not use locator calls enough. Popular locator calls include the crow, Canada goose, red-tailed hawk, peacock, pileated woodpecker, coyote and barred owl. The eight or nine notes of the barred owl has long been the most popular, especially just before dawn. But I have used most of the other calls with reasonable success. Using my voice for both barred owl calls and crow calls has been most effective for me; however, a goose call and a rabbit squealer have also worked well from after daylight through noontime.

Sometimes, switching locator calls may be just the ticket to making your first contact with a gobbler. Turkey sounds such as high-pitched yelping, cackling or gobbling will often elicit a shock gobble from a tom. If you are scouting before season definitely do not attempt to call the bird in. If you are hunting, get set up quickly and be prepared because that old longbeard may already be well on his way in.

THE KING OF SPRING

The resurrection of the wild turkey has been heralded as one of the greatest wildlife management successes. It is a credit to modern wildlife managers as well as the sportsmen who supported sound restoration programs and backed up that support with dollars. Farmers and landowners who nurtured newly transferred birds also deserve recognition.

In many places in America, hunters and non-hunters alike are enjoying the resurgence of our biggest game bird, the wild turkey. This magnificent creature deserves the admiration and respect of those who hunt him, as well as those who wish to observe or photograph him or just listen to his thunderous gobbling from high on a hardwood ridge on an early spring morning.

You've set yourself up strategically in a good spot, made some nice little yelps and a few clucks. Footsteps in the leaves! You level your shotgun in the general direction … there he is! Will your heart make it through one of hunting's most exciting moments? Of course. And you'll be back—again and again—for more.

Finding Wild Turkeys

There are five subspecies of the American wild turkey. While each kind of bird has similar physical features, they differ in coloration and certain other characteristics.

Eastern Wild Turkey
Meleagris gallopavo silvestris

The term *silvestris* means "of the woodlands." The Eastern wild turkey, once believed to require large unbroken stands of mature hardwood forests, now flourishes on a broad range of habitat from

Eastern gobbler.

northern Florida north through New England, southern Canada, west to Minnesota and Iowa, and south to Missouri and portions of Kansas, Oklahoma and Texas. Easterns generally occupy most of the eastern half of the United States.

Missouri leads the nation in harvest of Eastern wild turkeys, with approximately 56,000 birds annually during the spring season. Alabama, Georgia, Mississippi, Wisconsin, Pennsylvania, New York, Michigan, Iowa, Ohio and Tennessee each provide annual spring hunting harvests estimated between 20,000 and 50,00 birds.

Osceola Wild Turkey
Meleagris gallopavo osceola

The Osceola wild turkey, also known as the Florida, is named after the 19th century Seminole Chief Osceola. The Osceola is found only in the peninsula portion of the State of Florida. The Osceola is slightly smaller and darker in coloration than the Eastern, with more iridescent green and

Osceola gobbler.

red, and less bronze, than feathers of the Eastern. The Osceola is found in the flat pine woods adjacent to many large cattle ranches in Florida, and in the oak and palmetto hummocks and cypress swamps.

While much of Florida is in private land ownership, there are sizable wildlife management areas that harbor significant populations of the Osceola wild turkey.

Rio Grande Wild Turkey
Meleagris gallopavo intermedia

The Rio Grande wild turkey is found in the southwestern U.S. and northeastern Mexico. Its range extends through central Texas and the central plains states. The iridescent copper tones in the body feathers distinguish it from the Eastern and Osceola, as do the tail feathers and tail coverts that are tipped in a buff or tan rather than the

Rio Grande gobbler.

darker brown of the Eastern or Florida subspecies.

The Rio Grande inhabits brushy areas near stream- and riverbottoms as well as the mesquite, pine and scrub oak forests in the arid regions of the more open country in the central southwest. Texas undoubtedly has the most abundant populations of Rios, but for such a large state, public lands are extremely scarce. Both Kansas and Oklahoma are also good bets for taking a fine Rio Grande gobbler. You can also find Rios at lower elevations in Washington, Oregon, Colorado, Nevada, Wyoming, Utah, South Dakota, California, and they have also been transplanted to northern Idaho and Hawaii.

Merriam's Wild Turkey
Meleagris gallopavo merriami

Merriams gobbler.

The Merriam's wild turkey is a bird of the ponderosa pine foothills of the Rocky Mountains. Its historic range is believed to be Arizona, New Mexico and Colorado. It has been successfully introduced to areas north of its original range in the Rockies and to Washington, Oregon, California and Nebraska. Merriam's often migrate from the high elevations that they occupy during the spring, summer and early fall, to foothills and lower elevations during the winter. Merriam's are distinguished from Eastern, Rio Grande and Florida birds by their nearly white or ivory-colored feathers on their lower back, as well as the white tips of their tail coverts and tail feathers.

Many Western states bordering the Rockies offer Merriam's. To the east, North Dakota has both Easterns and Merriam's. South Dakota has Easterns, Merriam's and hybrids, and Nebraska has populations of Merriam's and hybrids. Recent information from the National Wild Turkey Federation reflects that Montana and Arizona offer only Merriam's wild turkeys, although extreme southern Arizona has non-huntable populations of Gould's wild turkey.

Gould's Wild Turkey
Meleagris gallopavo mexicana

Similar to the Merriam's, the Gould's is a bird of the mountains. Non-huntable populations of the Gould's are found in extreme southern Arizona and New Mexico. Huntable populations exist in northern Mexico.

The Gould's wild turkey is the largest of all the wild turkey subspecies. The distinctly white tips of the tail coverts and the terminal band of the tail feathers are wider than in the Merriam's. Body plumage has a blue-green iridescent cast. If you expect to add the Gould's wild turkey to your Grand Slam, you will have to travel to Mexico.

Gould's gobbler.

Chapter 14

Fall Turkeys: Hunting the Other Turkey

By Tom Carpenter

A warm, late-morning October sun lulled me into a pleasant half-sleep as I sat against the old oak tree.

A band of turkeys had entered this woodlot an hour ago, and I scrambled to circle ahead of the birds and set up. My occasional calling hadn't yet drawn any responses. I was just enjoying the morning and the colorful woods.

The initial adrenaline rush from seeing the big, beautiful turkeys was long gone.

Why limit your turkey hunting to springtime? Fall hunting offers an attraction all its own—from the chance to take a gobbler amidst all of autumn's glory (far left), to the fun of calling fall's bread-and-butter birds, the hens (left) and young-of-the-year birds. Any fall turkey you shoot is a good turkey!

But every 10 minutes or so I still called with hope. I opened my eyelids to stroke out a few more yelps on my box call—not too excited but nice and plaintive and a little tentative, as if to say, "I'm lonely, where are you?"

Soft yelps responded back, and you've never seen someone wake up so completely and so fast! I straightened up, shifted into position with shotgun at-the-ready on my knee, checked my head net, and picked up the box to call again.

Had I really heard a turkey? Or had I been dreaming? I called back in the tone and cadence I had heard, and got another answer—the distance was already cut in half! What to do? Call again? Before I could decide, several blue turkey heads appeared 50 or 60 yards down the ridge, bobbing toward me.

Blood pounded through my head so hard I thought it would blow a gasket out. The birds were coming!

Understanding Fall Turkeys

Fall is a time of transition for turkeys. Summer's broods have broken up, and the birds congregate into loose flocks of: hens and jennies (young hens); jakes (brothers of the jennies); broodless hens (though often they'll be with the hens and jennies); and gobblers (they'll stay in this group until spring).

A good hen will weigh 9 or 10 pounds, maybe as much as 12, a jennie 6 to 8. The young jakes will weigh at least as much as their mothers. Surprisingly, gobblers are lighter now than in the spring; they put on fat over the winter, in preparation for spring's extended mating work.

Turkeys will travel the countryside, working the food sources. Daily movement patterns will change with the weather and food. But find what they're eating (page 146) and they'll return, stoking up for the upcoming winter.

Fall turkeys "talk" more than you might think, using a variety of sounds (yelps, purrs, clucks and the classic kee-kees and kee-kee runs) to keep track of each other. You'll even hear an occasional half-gobble, especially from young jakes feeling their oats.

Many hunters target fall jakes—handsome young-of-the-year gobblers (with itty bitty beards) that love to talk with you as you call.

Autumn finds turkeys gathering together in different types of flocks: hens and their jennies; hens without young; jakes that have left their mothers and joined together; and bachelor, full-grown gobblers. Because the birds are grouped, and not spread across the landscape, they can be hard to find.

144

A Different Kind of Hunt

Fall turkey hunting doesn't get nearly the press that spring hunting does. And that's not surprising. There's so much else to do in the fall—deer hunting with bow and gun, other big game hunts, traditional bird and waterfowl hunting.

Sure, I still go ga-ga in spring, chasing lovelorn gobblers about the countryside. But fall turkeys fill a huge share of my hunting dreams throughout the year. I live, at least in part, for golden October days, the smell of fall fields and forests, the sight of shimmery-black turkeys feeding in the orange light of an autumn afternoon.

If you're willing to steal some time from all the other hunts that fill the season, fall turkeys are pure hunting fun. Game is abundant, with young-of-the-year birds pushing turkey numbers to their highest level of the year. The birds are often vocal, gregarious and responsive to calling. Plus if you get a bird, the eating is superb.

And it must be said: Any legal fall turkey is a good turkey. Young jakes and jennies will often come readily to a call; but don't get lackadaisical with your setup or camouflage, and don't fidget, or they will nail you. Adult hens are warier but abundant. These classes of birds make up the bulk of fall harvests. And a mature fall tom, his interests focused on survival and not procreating, is the supreme turkey hunting challenge.

Here are strategies and techniques for hunting them all, when the woods are alive with autumn's glory.

The traditional fall hunting method, and it is effective, is to scatter a flock and call birds back to your hidden, waiting gun (see sidebar page 147). But with limited acreage to hunt all fall— maybe access to a farm or two, or perhaps a hunt club or lease—who wants to make the turkeys extra spooky, or go scattering the turkeys off to someone else's land where they might regroup on their own and not need to come back? And on public land, you might push the birds to someone else's waiting gun.

So these techniques take a low-impact approach—more like deer hunting, but with some calling mixed in. This leaves the turkeys where you want them: calm and confident and on land you can hunt.

Scouting

Blah, blah, blah, scouting is boring. But scouting and woodsmanship are key to all these hunting strategies. Remember—you can also scout turkeys while you're scouting deer, bowhunting deer, hunting small game or pursuing other game birds.

You need to define what areas the turkeys are using for roosting, feeding, dusting, watering and just plain hanging out … and

Fall turkey hunting is a different kind of turkey hunting. You'll often find yourself setting up amongst color like this.

the general routes they're traveling between each.

Roosting. Be in the woods at fly-up time and listen for wingbeats. Search the forest floor for the feathers and droppings that indicate a roost tree. Know where your birds spend their nights.

Feeding. Hard mast—nuts and acorns—is important. Look for the scratchings that turkeys leave as they work the woods. Soft mast is key too—berries and fruits that ripen in fall. Harvested grainfields, especially corn and soybeans, will draw foraging turkeys; so will hayfields, pastures, meadows and clearings—for the green feed and insects (such as grasshoppers and ladybugs) there. Have a good idea of where turkeys are likely to feed in the mornings and afternoons.

Dusting. Look for small open areas of dry dirt that feature wing marks, scratchings and dropped feathers. This is where turkeys "dust" themselves. I annually find this evidence in one woodlot on a particular tractor trail; one year I will kill a turkey there.

Watering. Especially in the arid West, turkeys need water. But no matter where you hunt, "water" doesn't necessarily mean a true pond or stream. Springs and seeps provide plenty of water for a flock of fall turkeys.

Hanging out. Biologists call it loafing cover. I

Look for fall turkey food, including hard mast such as acorns (top left), waste grain such as corn (top right), oats or wheat, and soft mast such as berries or grapes (bottom two photos).

call it hanging out. Where do your turkeys spend their days?

Strategies for scouting. Fall turkeys can be exasperating and sometimes won't do the same thing day after day in this time of transition. But try to put together pieces of the birds' travels and routines, so you can put yourself in likely places. Actually walk the woods and fields. Look at the ground for turkey sign. If the terrain allows it, use your binoculars. Actually seeing turkeys feeding, moving, flying up to roost ... this is prime information for the hunt.

One of my best scouting strategies is a phone call to the landowner. Ask where the birds have been seen and at

Sometimes the best fall scouting of all is seeing turkeys themselves, and figuring out where they move and hang out at what times of day.

146

The Traditional Scatter

*H*ere's how the traditional fall "scatter" works.

Fall turkeys like the comfort and safety a group provides. So search out a flock, sneak as close as possible, then rush them in a raucous, hooligan's attempt to scatter the birds to the wind. Be safe—do this without your gun. You must get the birds to fly in all directions so that they have to call to one another to regroup.

Do a scatter any time, but busting a flock just before or after they have flown up for the night is prime; return in the morning and set up well before first light to call back the lonely, still-separated birds.

Sneak in as close as you can and run in, screaming and carrying on like a madman to scatter the birds far and wide in different directions. Be safe though—lay your gun down first.

If you have a fall turkey tag and like to hunt other game, keep your turkey gun at camp or in your vehicle. If you happen upon a flock, scatter it, hustle back for your turkey gun, return and set up.

Or if you're carrying a shotgun, just keep a full-choke tube and a couple turkey shells in your vest.

Set up at the scatter point, or nearby. Cut some small branches and build a little blind if you wish, wait anywhere from 15 to 30 minutes, then start calling. It's a trick to figure out exactly how long to wait before calling. Call too soon and the birds will be suspicious; call after the real hen(s) start and they will win.

Once the turkeys are scattered, set up, wait just a little while, and start calling them back. Exciting!

Use yelps and kee-kees. Throw in some plaintive, lost tones (yes, calling is an art). You might yelp to get a kee-keeing bird to come, or vice versa. Whatever gets birds calling back and coming to you, keep doing it!

You'll be surprised at how weak-kneed and breathless a 12-pound jake can make you, as he sneaks and bobs toward you through the forest with you watching over the rib of a shotgun barrel. Then it's up to you whether you'll be eating him or a sorry Butterball for Thanksgiving dinner.

what time of day. I also scout in the summer to see what crops are in which fields, what the upcoming mast crop might be like, and also just to see some turkeys and broods, and to get excited about turkey hunting.

LOW-IMPACT HUNTING STRATEGIES

So here you are, a fall turkey tag in your pocket. Some scouting homework has been completed, and you have an idea where the turkeys might be at what times.

Fall's turkey hunter must be versatile. No one technique is right all day long. Here are a variety of low-impact hunting strategies to add to your vest of tricks. Evaluate, pick-and-choose, modify—use these ideas as the bases for building your own fall strategy for the turkeys and countryside you hunt.

Coming off the Roost

Hunting turkeys off the roost isn't just for spring gobblers. If you have an idea where turkeys are roosting (or better yet, if you've actually seen them fly up), sneak as close as you dare the next morning, well before first light, and set up.

As fly-down time nears, make some sleepy clucks and soft yelps. In essence, you are the first bird down. Work the clucks and yelps, and try to lure the birds your way after they fly down. It helps to be set up between the roost and the place where the turkeys want to go.

Morning Setups

If your roost setup doesn't pan out, or you don't know where turkeys might be roosting, set up for a good morning sit. Select feeding areas now—the corner of a harvested crop field is great, as are meadows. Or set up where you've seen turkeys traveling, or at spots they're likely to pass: a point of timber, along a fenceline, beside a finger of brush, in a funnel area between woods, fields or hills.

I like to put out a decoy or two. Set them where they can be seen for some distance—to give a visual assurance to birds that decide to come to your calling, or to attract attention from birds that haven't heard you.

To call, make purrs and clucks. Belt out a few lonely yelps or kee-kees every so often, to get the attention of turkeys that might be passing out of sight. A gregarious bunch, fall turkeys will often come to investigate the calls or maybe to check out the newcomers (your decoys) who have invaded the territory.

If I feel good about a setup, I might stay all morning. Or I might move a couple times but spend at least an hour at each spot.

Hunting birds coming off roost isn't just for spring. Roost some birds the night before, get close to them before daylight, and call 'em in.

Spot, Get Ahead & Set Up

This is a good technique if you have strategic vantage points to watch from. The idea is to spot turkeys, observe them, and try to determine their expected travel route. This isn't always easy—they're turkeys—so make your best guess as to where they're going (this is where your scouting pays off). Then sneak there and set up.

Put out some decoys, get comfortable, make a few soft yelps. Don't call non-stop, but make some turkey sounds every few minutes or so. Purr and cluck a little bit in between yelps. This is the technique I used to get close to the turkeys that started this story.

Hunting open farm country, the author spotted a group of birds, snuck ahead, set up and called. It works!

Shotguns & Loads for Fall Turkeys

Shoot a pump or autoloader shotgun in 12 gauge or larger. You don't need anything fancy; a full choke is key, as is letting the birds get within 30 yards, preferably at 20 or so. Choke your barrel as tight as it goes—many new turkey chokes are now available.

Shot sizes from 4 to 6 are good for fall turkeys. I straddle the middle with No. 5 shot (1¾ ounces worth) in a 3-inch magnum shell. When I do my part, Winchester Supreme Turkey Loads have yet to fail me. Pack as much punch as your gun will take; turkeys are tough and you'll need it.

If you hunt spring turkeys, you're set—use the same gun and load in fall.

No matter what shotgun you use, two beads on a rib makes for extra good lining-up as you sight on a bird. Or use one of the turkey sights or scopes available. Shoot for the base of the turkey's head, where skin meets the feathers of the neck. That way your pattern, as it expands, can hit both vital areas: head and neck.

Use a 12 gauge gun (full choke of course) and load up with magnum shells carrying 1¾ ounces or more of No. 5 shot—it's a standard and deadly turkey load.

The hours right up until noon or so are all excellent, but after that, fall action can get slow. Sometimes it seems like the turkeys just disappear.

If the weather is good, there's nothing better than lazing away an Indian summer afternoon at a couple setups. Hunt in the "hanging out" cover you scouted, making setups for an hour or so each at pretty, strategic spots in the woods or whatever other cover the turkeys are using. Call with soft purrs and clucks, and yelp or kee kee occasionally to see if you can attract some attention or stir something up.

Set up in the timber in midday, call a little and wait. Now, patience is a fall turkey hunter's best virtue.

If the weather is unseasonably warm, an area with spring seeps or other dampness (such as a river- or creekbottom) could be a good bet. If the weather is horrible—windy or spitting snow for instance—go on the leeward side of hills, and into hollows—places where the wind isn't blowing.

Areas with hard mast are good in the afternoon too, to catch turkeys feeding under the forest cover. And don't overlook overgrown or fallow fields—turkeys can be surprisingly partial to this type of cover; set up along a fenceline or corner where woods or other cover meet the field.

In the late afternoon, move your setup back out to the more traditional feeding areas, in an attempt to intercept a flock on their afternoon feeding session.

This is fall's answer to spring's "Cutt & Run." The "Sneak & Yelp" is, essentially, a still-hunt through good turkey territory.

Move slowly and quietly—you're still-hunting—and stop every so often to call. You might spot turkeys to call to, before they spot you. Short of that, call blind at strategic spots every hundred yards or so. Stroke or blow out a few yelps; kee-kees are worth throwing in too. Sooner or later you'll get an answer.

A word of advice from one who knows: When calling blind, choose your position thoughtfully and know the answer to this question: "Am I safe? And how fast can I set up if a turkey calls back?"

Before you call, have your face mask up and lean against a tree, so you can simply drop down to your butt if a bird answers. Only if a turkey

Sneaking-and-yelping, fall's answer to spring's cutting-and-running, works. As you are in spring, be safe!

Fall Calling

Calling is integral to fall turkey hunting. As with most things, simpler is better. Here are the calls you'll need to know, and some suggestions as to which callers will best produce the sounds for you.

Yelp—The basic fall call. There are fancy names like "assembly yelps" and "lost yelps," but basically it's just yelping. Vary cadences, try different calls, go louder or softer to try to elicit responses. Basically, a yelp should get the attention of any turkeys in the vicinity. Boxes and slates are great, diaphragm calls will work too. If you get answers, call back using the tone and cadence you hear. If you're after gobblers, call only sparingly and try to replicate their lower, raspier voices; only yelp two or three times at a crack.

Kee-Kee—The whistling half-yelp of a lost, adolescent bird looking for its flock. It actually consists of three notes (kee-kee-kee) and occasionally four. **Kee-kee runs** are most often made by the young-of-the-year jakes; a kee-kee run adds a couple not-so-hot yelps to the end of a kee-kee (kee-kee-kee-yelp-yelp). Aggressive fall calls, these sounds ask for a response and will bring in birds of all ages. Best produced on a diaphragm call.

Fall calling is an art of its own, but you can use the callers you have for spring hunting: box, peg-and-slate, diaphragm, push button and others.

Purr and Cluck—The little sounds of contented turkeys. Turkeys are always talking, and they expect noise from other turkeys (your decoys), so these calls add important sound and realism to any setup scene. Slates are good, and so are diaphragms.

Fighting Purrs—Try mimicking a turkey fight. Use a diaphragm, and put one of the push-button fighting purr callers, or a slate or box, to work at the same time. You want to sound like two different and agitated turkeys going at it. Some curious birds might come running to see or get in on the action, as turkeys (especially rambunctious fall jakes) are always working to establish dominance and a pecking order.

Scratching—At a setup in the woods, don't be afraid to scratch some leaves on the forest floor occasionally, making the sounds of feeding turkeys. Use three fingers or a stick, flicking leaves back in the manner a feeding, scratching turkey would.

sounds far enough out should you risk setting up a decoy.

One hot fall day, I was sneaking and yelping and had covered a lot of ground. Tired, I stopped at the mouth of a small hollow, took a step into the cool and shady woods, and yelped. "Yawk, yawk, yawk" was the immediate answer, and the bird was not far away.

I had to creep forward to find a suitable tree to set up against—and the bird was already coming. Of course, it boogered. All I saw was a black-feathered bullet snaking away through the timber. Had I been thinking positively, expecting a response, I would have had a chance.

In late afternoon, set up along turkeys' travel routes to their roosts.

Getting on the Roost

The afternoon has passed and the sun is sinking. Sneak into a roost area, set up, and wait for the birds. Be ready at least an hour before sunset. You want everything to be quiet and calm. Put out a couple decoys. Do some light purring and clucking—like you're an early bird already in the bedroom.

The goal is to make the roost area appear safe. Soft calling enhances that perception and could attract turkeys that are in the area but not necessarily heading toward your little arena. Don't call too loudly or aggressively. In the calm of an evening, your soft little mumbles, whines and purrs will be plenty loud.

FALL'S REWARD

Back to the hunt that started this story.

The turkeys kept coming as I watched over the shotgun's barrel. A diaphragm call was at-the-ready in my mouth, but I probably couldn't have used it anyway, my mouth was so dry from excitement. No matter. The birds had heard enough and were on their way—not at a run, but the blue heads bobbed through October's leaves at a steady pace.

At a range of 18 yards, the first turkey stepped into an opening and stopped. Did I want a hen, or a jake if there was one? Was this a young bird or an adult? A young one would be great, not hurt the flock. Too late. The bird made the decision and stepped through.

The next head moved in, periscoped up, and turkeys flushed in every direction at the sound of

Autumn's finest prize: a good turkey called in fair and square through blazing autumn woods.

my shot. "[Expletive.] Missed!"

But of course I would see a bunch of escaping birds—there were 5 or 6 altogether. So I jumped up and stumbled over on bloodless, stiff legs—hoping against hope—and pounced on the big, gorgeous adult hen that had fallen at the shot.

When she was still, I laid her in the leaves and arranged her ruffled feathers. I sat back and admired them as they glistened a hundred shades of bronze and green and russet and purple in the October sun, the forest alive with fall around me, as happy as I imagine I ever could be.

Finding Fall Turkeys

*F*all turkey hunting is nowhere near as popular as the spring hunt. And that's just how we fall turkey addicts like it! But frankly, with all birds fair game, limited hunting is good. Shoot too many hens and the population will suffer. So not every state or turkey management unit offers a fall season. In some states you have to draw a fall tag, just like spring.

Where's the best place to hunt? Your own state, and your own spots—if a season is open. If you're thinking

The author and his father with a hen and jake taken on a golden October day in Wisconsin's southwestern hill country.

about traveling, consider some of the great spring destinations—Missouri, Alabama, Texas. Sleeper states include West Virginia and Virginia with strong fall traditions, as well as New York and Pennsylvania. A nice idea—tack a turkey hunt onto a Western big game or bird hunt if the timing's right—South Dakota, Wyoming, Montana, Colorado and Idaho all come to mind.

Chances are, you'll be hunting in or around the hard-woods. No matter what kind of bird—hen, jake or jenny—that you get working to your calls, you've had a good hunt. Gobblers can be shot too, but that's less of a calling game and more of a deep-cluck-and-wait or raspy-yelp-or-two-and-wait game.

In some states, you can hunt turkeys with a dog. A turkey dog finds the birds, scatters them, comes back and obediently hides with you at your setup. Then you work the birds in an attempt to call them back. A tall order, but tons of fun when it works … and it's high entertainment to watch Fido try to make the retrieve!

Chapter 15

BOBWHITE QUAIL: TIMELESS BIRD HUNTING TRADITION

BY JIM CASADA

O ver time, adoring hunters and sporting scribes have gifted the bobwhite quail with many names. Mr. Bob, Gentleman Bob, the Noble Quail and others are among them. But as South Carolina writer Havilah Babcock put it, "call him Bob White, quail, bird or whatever you will in the rest of the country . . . to elder sportsmen of the South, this saucy little patrician is still a partridge. It is *lese majeste* to call him anything else."

Over the years, bobwhite quail (far left and left) have stolen the hearts of untold scores of bird hunters. Bobwhites are tiny (cocks and hens alike weigh only 5 or 6 ounces) but they are beautiful to behold both in flight as your shotgun tries to catch up to their whirring covey flush ... and in the palm of your hand a few moments later as you admire their intricate plumage.

Babcock and a host of other writers have sung the praises of this feathered five ounces of flying dynamite, and with good reason. Hunting the bobwhite quail brings the best of that timeless connection between a man and his dog. And the sporty nature of the brave quail is, at least to Southern eyes, of a class in itself. As Robert Ruark once suggested, "I never knew a man that hunted quail who didn't come out of it a little politer by comparison," and the sport has always been one with overtones of gentility. Unfortunately, much of the lore and some of the lure of the bobwhite belongs to a world that we are rapidly losing.

STORIED PAST, TROUBLED PRESENT

Arguably no type of American hunting has a richer tradition. The vision of a pointer locked tight against the horizon as the sun sets, or frozen in place amidst a million diamonds of frost on a chilly December morning, is an enduring one. Then too, the gregarious nature of the bird, found

155

Understanding Bobwhites

A hen bobwhite (left) has a buff-colored throat and eyepatch compared to the cock's white markings (right).

During the early fall and on through hunting season, bobwhites live together in groups known as coveys. These groups offer security, but the birds separate as winter gives way to spring and the mating season arrives. This is when the bobwhite is most vocal, using the mating call from which its name is derived, but the bird has other sounds in its vocabulary as well. You can use the reassembly call to locate singles after a covey has been flushed.

Once the birds pair up, as long as two weeks to a month may pass before the hen and cock begin nesting. Ground nesting birds that build in a variety of sites, bobwhites prefer areas with heavy undergrowth, such as broomsedge fields. Their nests are almost always positioned in thick cover conveniently adjacent to openings such as old logging roads or field edges. Once the nest has been constructed, the hen normally lays an egg a day until the set is complete; the average number of eggs is around 14. Incubation takes just longer than three weeks and, in some cases the cock will help with incubation.

A brooding period of some two weeks follows, but from day one the chicks feed themselves. Insects such as grasshoppers, rich in protein, are crucial during the early stages of development, but all sorts of seeds, berries, and vegetation also form part of their diet.

Chicks can fly at about two weeks of age and by two months flush with alacrity and fly rapidly to cover. Before they are able to fly, chicks immobilize with warning sounds from their parents and can instantly become almost invisible. By the time they reach 15 weeks of age, the chicks are full grown and independent. Still, autumn coveys typically come from a family of quail, but individual birds or two groups will often join to form a covey too. The birds roost on the ground in a circle, with all heads facing outwards. A pile of droppings is a telltale index to a roost site, and unless disturbed, coveys will often roost in the same general area night after night.

Bobwhite range.

in coveys, adds to its appeal. To quote Babcock once again, "the tense second before a whopping covey explodes is the most nerve-racking silence in history."

For a few shining decades in the sun, the bobwhite was incredibly abundant. All sorts of considerations worked in its favor. Farming practices of the "40 acres and a mule" type, where clean farming was unknown, meant overgrown ditch banks and fencerows for cover, unharvested peafield corners, controlled burning and other agricultural methods that helped the quail.

Then too, tenant farmers trapped, shot, or killed many of the quail's enemies—'coons, skunks, 'possums and snakes—on sight. Every raptor was a "chicken hawk" and thus considered a prime candidate for lead poisoning. Fire ants had not yet begun their inexorable march northward, use of pesticides such as DDT was limited, and farmed-out croplands left idle over vast expanses of the South provided ideal quail habitat.

I grew up at the tag end of the quail's heyday, which stretched roughly from shortly before the Great Depression into the early 1960s. Although my homeland was not prime quail territory, at least in comparison with the longleaf pine and broomsedge terrain of much of the Southland's piedmont region, bobwhites were nonetheless incredibly plentiful. Seldom did I go rabbit hunting without flushing half a dozen or more coveys; individuals such as my uncle, who raised pointers, fully expected to find anywhere from a dozen to 20 coveys in the course of a day's outing.

Those days are now gone forever. The unpaid gamekeepers we knew as tenant farmers have given way to huge machines that farm every square foot of available land. Hawks, which can and do wreak havoc on quail, are protected and abundant. No one traps anymore, with subsistence trapping having given way to the price of furs plummeting in the face of political correctness. Controlled burns are reduced or canceled by

If the countryside isn't farmed fence-to-fence, it has a chance to be quail country. The birds thrive "on the edge" of agriculture; but to support bobwhites there must be grassland, fencerows, thickets, pastures and other untilled land.

concerns about air pollution; fire ants seem to be everywhere; and for every friend it has, the brave little bobwhite seems to face a hundred enemies. In some areas where the quest for quail was once the most popular type of hunting, the bobwhite's numbers in the wild are so low biologists talk of them vanishing within a decade. Elsewhere they hang on, albeit in sharply reduced numbers.

OF QUAIL & DOGS

Still, much of the magic remains, for even in its finest hour quail hunting was never a numbers game. Instead, it was a sport for the soul, one that reached its full consummation through the understanding between a man and his dog.

The argument over what type of dog is best suited for quail hunting is an interminable one without any real answer. I'm a pointer man myself, and I find no fault with Havilah Babcock's thoughts on the matter: "A gracefully pointing dog is to me a perennial delight—a scene which, however often beheld, has always a newness about it, one which never fails to bring me a quickening of the senses and a long moment's rapture." But setters have equally staunch advocates, and I'll leave attempted resolution of the pointer vs. setter debate to the liar's bench or world diplomacy.

Suffice it to say that if ever a game bird was made for bird dogs, it is the quail. It is possible to find and flush the occasional covey without canine assistance, and you might even locate the odd single after a covey rise. Still, you will find far more game, get far better shots and lose far fewer birds with the staunch assistance of a canine companion. You will also enjoy the unquestioning friendship of a fellow hunter who never questions your wisdom and worships you as if you were a god. A good bird dog is one of the great joys in the sporting life, and therein, I strongly suspect, lies the key explanation of the enduring, indeed, eternal appeal of quail hunting.

HUNTING STRATEGIES

Good dogs will, to a considerable degree, take care of matters once they are on the ground, and as Robert Ruark once suggested, "if he's got sense enough to be bred from a family with a nose and a sense of decency, any mistake you let him make is your fault." Ruark continued: "There ain't nothing anybody can tell a good dog that the dog don't know better than the man. It's the dog's business to know his business." Those are true words from one of the sport's great sages. But the fact remains that sensible hunters can make a world of difference by bringing tactical considerations into their quail hunting.

Anyone who has fooled with wild bobwhites in the last two decades realizes that the birds won't be too far removed from a near-impenetrable hellhole. Furthermore, that's where the birds will almost certainly fly when flushed. It helps to realize that most feeding takes place fairly early in the morning

Good quail hunting is as much about good dog-work as anything else.

158

Guns & Loads for Bobwhites

Light loads (No. 7½ or 8 shot), open barrels (often in a double gun) and smaller gauges (16, 20 or 28) comprise the traditional bobwhite quail setup.

Traditionally, double barrels were the gun of choice for bobwhites, although even in the heyday of Mr. Bob, when coveys were big and often numbered 15 or 20 birds, plenty of hunters opted for semiautomatics or "corn shuckers" (pumps). Using either of the latter two guns, some seasoned hunters could get off four or five shots on a covey rise, especially if the birds did not take flight all at once. These were 12, 16 or 20 gauges, although "sporting gentlemen" showed a distinct preference for a 16 or 20 gauge.

Light loads and wide-open chokes were the way to go, with 7½ or 8 shot and skeet or cylinder bores getting preference. Most shots were within 30 yards. Then, as the numbers of wild birds declined and the remaining bobwhites became much more prone to "flush wild," this changed. Many shots occurred at distances of 40 yards or even more, which placed a premium on tighter chokes and heavier loads with 7½ or even 6 shot. In such circumstances, side-by-side or over-under barrel lovers enjoyed a certain advantage, as they had a selection of choke for a second, longer shot.

Interestingly, in today's quail hunting, which is with rare exceptions done on preserves and involves pen-reared birds, hunters have returned to their roots. Light loads, more open barrels and sporty 20, 28 or .410 gauge guns are commonly encountered. To an appreciable degree, guns and loads for quail have always been a matter of personal preference, though for me I'll always envision whopping bevies of bobs taking wing before an elderly gentleman who handles a Parker or Fox 16 or 20 gauge with the sort of intimate familiarity born of long practice. The gun movement is so smooth, and the wing-shooting so sure, that the little double barrel seems to be an extension of the hunter's body.

When they've been pressured a little bit, bobwhites have absolutely no qualms about retreating to thick, brushy, nasty places.

offer fairly predictable action, and if the operation is run the way it should be, the birds will be strong fliers that present a solid challenge to both hunter and dog.

BOBWHITE MAGIC

In the case of the grand little gentleman known as the bobwhite, the "good old days" were truly just that. It was a time when, to hunters, the night before opening day seemed longer than the week before Christmas, when every little piece of acreage had a home covey, and when a man was judged by the dogs he raised and his willingness to let his hunting partner claim a bird when both hunters shot simultaneously. Some of that is gone forever, but it is still possible to enjoy the performance of a skilled dog, to know the inner glow of a clean double and to savor the sweetness of a sunset covey. Such is the mesmerizing magic of the bobwhite.

(though not at daybreak) and in the last hour of daylight. During those times, a dog is most apt to find a covey out in the open in the sort of situation likely to present decent shots.

Also take into consideration scenting conditions. Days of high winds, unseasonably hot weather or extremely dry conditions all work against top-level performance by dogs. It also helps to make things easier for your dogs. That means changing the "dogs on the ground" frequently and making sure they drink plenty of water.

Positioning on points can make a great deal of difference when it comes to the likelihood of getting a decent shot. When dealing with wild birds, you don't want to dally when a dog does point.

In truth, most folks who now hunt bobwhite quail, not to mention those who plan to do so, need to keep preserve birds in mind. They

When you're hunting bobwhites and the dog goes on point, get there now!

Finding Bobwhites

You can still find wild bobwhites today (left), where the land is managed carefully and with an eye toward wildlife. But much hunting is done on preserves (right), and the experience here can be great.

The Southeast, from the Virginias to Texas, has always been the best-known bobwhite territory. But the birds are also found in the Midwest and in portions of the mid-Atlantic states. Today, sadly, over virtually all of its range, the bobwhite is in serious trouble. A host of interrelated factors, which are discussed in more detail elsewhere in this story, explain the situation.

Portions of Texas and Oklahoma, especially in years when there is decent rainfall, are a noteworthy exception to the general tale of decline, and there are still goodly numbers of wild bobs on intensively managed plantations in south Georgia, Low Country South Carolina, and elsewhere.

For the most part though, old-time hunters who remember the glory days of the 1940s and '50s, when 20-covey days were common, now have to content themselves with covering a lot of ground to find two or three coveys in a day of hunting. Even then, the odds are about 50/50 that any given covey will flush wild.

Where it still remains, a blend of agricultural, fallow and brushy land makes the best bobwhite country. Grain fields are important for the food

that waste grain produces. Fallow, grassy land provides nesting and loafing cover that is safe from the plow and hay mower. And woods and brush provide the framework of hiding cover necessary for the bobwhite's escape from predators and bad weather.

All this translates into one of two options for hunters: Spend a lot of money to gain access to one of the places where there are still wild quail, or hunt pen-raised birds on a preserve. The latter option can be quite appealing if the operation is properly managed. With call-back systems, preseason releases, the planting of birds reared in flight pens with no contact with humans, and other techniques can produce strong flying birds that quite closely duplicate the wild bird experience. For the average hunter, increasingly, preserve shooting is the way to go. It is virtually a must for dog training, because there is no substitute for contact with lots of birds when it comes to the making of a good dog. Or, as Babcock put it, "nothing in the wide world and all the libraries therein will substitute for birds in training a bird dog."

The Literature of the Bobwhite
by Jim Casada

For reasons that remain elusive but are nonetheless real, the bobwhite has been the focus of some of the finest outdoor literature America has produced. Perhaps it is the magic of a rangy pointer working his canine wizardry as he ranges across a field of broomsedge asparkle with a million diamonds of frost on a chilly December morning. Or maybe it is the ever-returning rush of excitement occasioned by a whopping covey taking wing so close the hunter can almost touch them.

What could be finer than a brace of beautiful quail on a fine fall day? Through the years, many writers have touted the virtues of bobwhites and bobwhite hunting.

Nor should the gentility which is an integral part of the sport's roots be overlooked.

Whatever the explanation, quail hunting has produced a rich outpouring of wonderful writing. The list that follows is but a sampling at best, but the collective work of the quartet of authors mentioned does provide something of a road map to cherished hours of armchair adventure.

South Carolina's Havilah Babcock has been described, with considerable justice, as the poet laureate of the partridge (as he insisted quail be called). An English professor who wrote as a way of dealing with chronic insomnia, he lived for bird season. Indeed, the titles of two of his books, *My Health Is Better in November* (when quail season opened) and *I Don't Want to Shoot an Elephant*, suggest as much. His other collections of stories include *The Best of Babcock, Jaybirds Go to Hell on Friday*, and *Tales of Quails 'n Such*. Babcock also wrote one full-length book (as opposed to anthologies bringing together his stories), *The Education of Pretty Boy*. Bevies of bobwhites, tales of canine companions and large measures of good humor spice all his tales.

Tennessee's Nash Buckingham also sang the praises of the quail in dozens of stories. As is the case with Babcock, most of Buckingham's work first appeared as articles in major outdoor magazines and subsequently found its way into anthologies. There are several quail hunting stories in Buckingham's books, which include *De Shootinest Gent'man, Mark Right, Game Bag, Blood Lines, Tattered Coat, Hallowed Years*, and *Ole Miss'*. Buckingham was a master of dialect, and his tales are redolent of a world we have lost—one of vast plantations, the sort of wealth which lent itself to hunting in style, mint juleps on the veranda, and an understanding between those of Mr. Buck's ilk and the "black huntermen" who were his constant companions.

Archibald Rutledge was also a master of dialect.

While he devoted much of his vast outpouring of sporting literature to deer and turkey hunting, he also penned many stories on birds (to anyone from the South, "bird" means quail). These are liberally sprinkled through dozens of books, including his best-known works such as *An American Hunter, Days Off in Dixie, Tom and I on the Old Plantation, Plantation Game Trails, Those Were the Days*, and *Bolio and Other Dogs*. I have collected many of Rutledge's finest pieces on dogs and bird hunting together in *Bird Dog Days, Wingshooting Ways*, and there are also a number of pieces of this genre in a second work I edited, *Hunting and Home in the Southern Heartland: The Best of Archibald Rutledge*.

Finally, no excursion into the world of quail hunting would be complete without mention of Robert Ruark. Arguably the finest outdoor writer this country has ever produced, this staunch son of the North Carolina soil included a number of bird hunting stories in his two best-known works on the outdoors, *The Old Man and the Boy* and *The Old Man's Boy Grows Older*. To read these pieces is to understand the magic that the interaction between a man, a dog, and a five-ounce bird can produce.

Much research has focused on the bobwhite, but the two enduring standards in the field are Herbert L. Stoddard's *The Bobwhite Quail* and Walter Rosene's *The Bobwhite Quail*.

For such a small package, bobwhite quail have attracted a large and loyal following. Bobwhites have been, and continue to be, the bird of many hunters' dreams.

Chapter 16

DESERT QUAIL: UNTAMED RENEGADES OF THE SOUTHWEST

BY PATRICK MEITIN

The untamed renegades of the desert quail gang are delicately beautiful creatures that live in some harshly beautiful country. Members include the Gambel's quail (opposite page), the scaled quail (also known as the blue quail in some locales, far left, this page), and the Montezuma quail (alias Mearn's quail, left).

I attended college "Back East," which is West Texas when you live in the desert Southwest. Consequently, I have spent some happily productive days in bobwhite country. This is why I can easily understand the cult status afforded Gentleman Bob as a game bird. He behaves as a man with pointing dogs would have him, proves relatively predictable day to day, and plays by a set of rules etched permanently in classic sporting literature.

I understand all this and respect it, certainly. But I prefer those untamed, renegade desert quail found in the wandering arroyos of the Southwest with its long Western vistas, cold nights and warm days.

Desert quail are an enigma—delicate in stature, austere in garish color schemes—yet they inhabit a land of stark drabness and harsh existence.

Take the Gambel's: buff and maroon, face of white-edged black, wearing that ostentatious top notch. The Montezuma (a.k.a. Mearn's, Harlequin, or fool's quail) appears so silly and pudgy with its oddly painted clown's face, brushy crest and nape, but so beautiful in a white-on-black spotted body.

165

Even a scaled quail, called "blue" or "cotton top" in some portions of its range, appears as fine and delicate as a classic Atlantic salmon fly, with its sharp-edged markings as fine as the flanks of a trophy tarpon.

Of course, hunting carries time-worn perceptions that are as difficult to shake as old home remedies for the common cold, an example being those who reject the quail of the desert out of hand without first being properly introduced to them. The myths are that these quail are unsporting types unwilling to hold for pointing dogs, unrefined and unruly once prodded into flight.

But to change your mind you need only labor into rough desert mountains to discover the steel-nerved Montezuma, properly scatter a covey of Gambel's into a bowl of low desert shrub, or venture far from the beaten path in search of scalies who are more prone to sit than run. If you can combine these things with a special, adaptable form of dog work, you too will discover and come to love the quail of the desert.

GAMBEL'S QUAIL

The Gambel's is one of the West's most widely distributed quail species, common through Arizona and southwest New Mexico, with populations as far flung as southeastern Utah, west central Colorado, extreme southern Nevada, southwest California and into northwest Sonora, Mexico.

Gambel's habitat includes environs where brush and cactus arroyos provide cover from birds of prey and predators, and where water is available. Gambel's are typically found in large coveys of from 20 to 45 birds, with bigger mobs not out of the question. When you find one Gambel's there are likely more of them nearby.

Discovering the most productive Gambel's hunting means walking away from roads and exploring draws and washes that are either too desolate or require too much effort to be investigated by the average nimrod. You'll often be wandering under a hot sun, so carry a daypack filled with snacks and water bottles. You need to get off the beaten path to find the best shooting. Land in the right place at the right time, when your dog is working at its best, and you might be surprised at how fast a limit of 10 or 15 birds can go into the game bag. Of course, you must do your part and hit the little rockets first!

Dogs for Gambel's

A bird dog is especially welcome in this trade, if contributing nothing more than retrieving downed birds or running cripples. A downed Gambel's can be difficult to put a hand to, especially in thick cover, and winged birds are notorious for running hard.

A sharp-nosed, well-trained canine friend is also a boon on the hunting end. Superior canine nose and stamina can help pare down vast desert territory to manageable size, helping get you into more birds.

To find Gambel's quail, get away from roads and any kind of beaten path. These birds like their seclusion.

Look for Gambel's quail in brushy, cactusy places. You will have to wade right in after them to make them fly. Note that Gambel's need some standing water in the vicinity; that should help narrow your search for birds.

Don't become frustrated if your Eastern pointing breed reared on ideal scenting conditions and well-behaved bobwhites acts a little confused when first put down in the desert. There is simply less scent in dry country, and desert birds are more apt to scoot out from under a steady point. A good pointer or setter will get the hang of it given a little time. This said, I would rather hunt behind a flusher while chasing Gambel's, not just because those dogs fit my temperament, but also because they are better able to adjust to the sometimes shifty nature of the game.

Now let's not get the idea that Gambel's are not willing to stick tight. A large group of Gambel's busted well and scattered into an open bowl or close-cropped hillside can easily put an Eastern bob to shame, and give your gun dog a chance to show off its stuff. A good covey break is what makes these situations happen. Get aggressive upon observing a large Gambel's rabble running ahead of you, as they are most often wont to do when in tight formations. Charge them! Invite the dog into the fray, shoot into the air (or the covey if they are within range); scatter them to the points of the compass. It helps at this point to mark your birds carefully. They will almost always fly uphill from the bottom where you've located them. Then it's time to see how good of a nose your pooch owns.

Even with a dog, scattered Gambel's are easy to walk right over. The dry, dusty desert offers the most difficult of scenting conditions, and the best desert quail dogs are usually born in it. Keep your dog well watered to keep its nose in good working order; this is usually easy, as stock tanks and windmills are also the places that concentrate Gambel's quail.

The later into a season you hunt, the more difficult quail seem to be to locate, though this is tied directly to hunting pressure. The best advice is to work near water, as quail congregate in these places. Walk out draws above and below obvious water sources to make the best of your efforts.

Understanding Desert Quail

Desert animals are ultimately regulated by fickle rains that visit during winter and later summer. Should these desert rains fail, the animals suffer. This is never more true, more critical, than with the quail of the desert. Not only must they receive moisture to thrive, but they must receive it during the right times of the year.

Winter rains are important to promote new growth that nesting mothers will need for egg production, succulent new shoots full of required nutrition, as well as grass cover to hide nests from prowling predators. But too much rain, or a blanketing snow late in the year, can cause birds to die from exposure.

After successful nesting, summer monsoons become all-important to create healthy populations of forbs and insects that chicks need while they are growing quickly. Conversely, too much rain too soon can flood nests, or subject newly hatched chicks to wet and cold that will cause exposure death. Gambel's and scalies, having failed at a first attempt at nesting, will lay a second clutch, but seldom a third.

When everything comes off perfectly, quail abound. One small slip of nature, and an entire year's crop can be lost overnight.

Hunting mortality does not affect overall health of quail populations. By increasing harvest you also decrease natural mortality and increase health among survivors; those remaining live longer and are healthier. Studies have shown that populations arrive at winter levels with or without hunting.

All quail can metabolize water from food, but they do take advantage of standing water when it is available. Quail have a crop that allows them to quickly gather food; then they hide while digesting it. Gambel's nest during late May and June, and will often produce two clutches of up to 10 eggs during a good year. Young hatch covered in down, or "precocially," and can walk as soon as they are hatched, then fly within a couple weeks. Quail form coveys, or large social groups, and breeding pairs stick together the entire breeding season; males mate with but one female.

Gambel's Quail

Standing 10 to 11½ inches tall, the Gambel's is characterized by a black, tear-shaped top-notch, found only on Gambel's and the valley (California) quail, a close relative. This top-notch is

Gambel's quail cock (background) and hen (foreground).

more pronounced on males than females, and males are also more boldly colored, with maroon flanks, white eye-like markings and a cream belly with a black smudge. The Gambel's ranges from central New Mexico westward across Arizona and just into southeastern California, and from northwestern Old Mexico to as far north as southeast Utah and west central Colorado.

In large groups Gambel's use a safety-in-numbers approach and run from danger, though scattered birds use camouflage to hide. Coveys of up to 50 birds are not uncommon. Calls are a three-syllabled "qua-quer'go" or "Chi-ca'go," and also light clucking notes.

Scaled Quail

The 10- to 12-inch-tall scaled quail, sometimes called "cotton top" because of the white crest atop its head, runs slate gray to blue in color. They are also sometimes

Scaled quail.

called blues because of this coloration. Their breast feathers are distinctly scaled, providing its most common namesake. Scalies nest in May and June, laying clutches of up to 10 eggs, and often twice during a season if moisture is sufficient.

Females have a white eye stripe and more distinct throat patch than males. Scalies prefer desert grasslands and brush, and are found from south Texas and central Old Mexico to as far north as southeastern Colorado, and as far west as east central Arizona. They have strong legs and prefer to run from threats instead of fly, traveling in coveys of up to 30 birds. Their voice is a guinea-hen-like "chekar'" or "pay-cos."

Montezuma Quail

The 8- to 9½-inch-tall Montezuma has gone through many name changes. Montezuma is the

Montezuma quail hen (background) and cock (foreground).

name scientific types have settled on today, but the bird has been called Mearn's recently, Harlequin if you have been around longer.

Montezumas prefer oak forests and wooded mountain slopes with abundant bunch grass between 1,000 and 3,000 feet elevation, but they regularly wander higher and are often observed as high as 10,000 feet.

The Montezuma is a squat, rotund quail with distinctive clown-like face markings and black flanks brightly spotted with white. Unlike Gambel's and scaled quail, which are primarily seed eaters, Montezumas eat rooted tubers almost exclusively. They sport oversized feet and claws for digging.

Montezumas are highly sensitive to overgrazing, and this has become a major contention between game managers and public-land ranchers. Montezumas must have grass cover to enjoy successful nesting, though they will delay nesting until summer rains arrive. As a result, they will often nest successfully when Gambel's or scaled quail have failed. They lay only one clutch of 3 to 5 eggs per season. Montezumas rely on their camouflage markings to hide from danger, instead of running or flying. They are found in coveys of up to 15 birds. Their voice is a soft, whinnying or quavering cry often described as ventriloquial in nature.

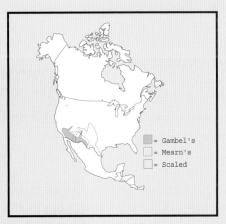

Desert quail range.

Though their plumage is less flashy than that of their Gambel's and Montezuma cousins, scalies have a subtle and refined beauty all their own.

SCALED QUAIL

You might hear hunters refer to the scaled quail by other names depending on where you are hunting. Where they are found in south and west Texas, locals might call them "cotton tops," while populations found from border to border in New Mexico might go by "blues." Scaled quail also live in eastern Arizona and southeastern Colorado where "scalies" is most often their handle.

No matter where they reside or what you call them, scaled quail are unpredictable when compared to the Gambel's. Water is still an important ingredient to success, but scalies seem less dependent on it than other desert quail species. Open grasslands and scattered chaparral brush pulls these true desert denizens farther from water, and they just don't seem as partial to the predictably crowded vegetation that often concentrates Gambel's.

This said, the hunter is still wise to keep water in mind when hunting scalies, if for no other reason than that you have little other choice in the vastness of the Southwest. Scaled quail are just as often found side by side with Gambel's, when the fancy strikes them to haunt brush. You just never know with scalies.

The scalie's reputation as a sprinter is not wholly unjustified. Growing up in eastern New Mexico, we knew nothing else so took them for what they were. This is to say we made the best of the situation. Quail hunting there simply meant doing what it took to adjust to what the species demanded.

I can recall a horrible amount of ground sluicing going on back then, but we were bloodthirsty youngsters, and what youngster is not prone to such indiscretions? There were no dogs involved to get caught in the crossfire, so we were endangering no one. Then we discovered quail dogs and found what scalie hunting could really be like!

Desert Runners

The scalies' tendency to run is directly proportional to the amount of shooting the birds

Look for scaled quail in open grassland scattered with chaparral and other brush. These quail aren't as partial to thick places as Gambel's are, and you'll also find scalies farther from water.

have received. In easily accessible cover that witnesses regular hunting pressure, getting a scalie into the air can be wholly frustrating, and you can hardly blame him.

A fresh covey of scalies is another story, inclined to behave just as a Gambel's would: Scatter a scalie covey well into open cover, then encourage Fido forward to do his thing on the singles and doubles.

Of course, who's to know if they are dealing with naïve birds or pressured scalies? With this in mind, it's normally best to hustle to busted birds, just in case. Scalies may wait courteously for your arrival, or flow over the next ridge while you're not looking.

No matter what kind of scalies you might discover—well-mannered or sprinter—a dog is a welcome hunting partner. A dog picks up your birds (which can look an awful lot like the ground they fall to), and is a must on inevitable running cripples. The best dog can nab the runners before they make too much ground.

Busting a determined covey of ground-loving scalies can require some effort. This includes a lot of jogging in most cases, and it is not considered bad etiquette in scalie hunting to shoot into a tight knot of sprinting birds to give them a boost into the air. If you take a pair from the ground you can be consoled by the fact that they do make the best kind of eating and no one will know the difference when they emerge from the skillet.

Of course, you might be like one friend of mine who would turn in his scattergun before he would ground-shoot any bird. He prefers to shoot his scattering shots into the air. To each his own. Any way you look at it, the best blue quail hunters are those with long legs and strong lungs.

A Montezuma in your hand is like a little blessing from the desert wilderness.

Montezuma Quail

There was a time, within my lifetime, when game managers believed the Montezuma quail—some call them Mearn's, Harlequins or fool's quail—were quite scarce, as few hunters had actually observed them in the wild. I used to believe the same, having only observed a small group here and there while pursuing some sort of big game, mostly Coues' whitetail, in Arizona or New Mexico.

There came a day when I decided, rare or not, I must have a Montezuma for a collection of mounted quail I had gathered over the years. I hiked far into a wilderness region, followed by my Gambel's-tuned Lab, to where I had hunted Coues' deer, and stepped on a few Montezumas. What I found changed my perspective completely.

Not only were the birds quite plentiful, but my Lab, Kody, found them on nearly every ridge with suitable habitat. I soon discovered they were just as plentiful closer to home, sans a wilderness trek. I would also learn just how tight these burly quail hold, and why you'll seldom see them without a gun dog's assistance.

Tight Sitters

It does not matter where you find them. If a setter or pointer rigidly locked on a bird takes your breath away, the Montezuma is the desert quail for you. Put the average Montezuma and a pen-raised bobwhite side by side, send in the dog, and I'd put my money on the Montezuma to flush last every time.

I remember a particular incident, watching Kody become obviously "birdy" with his telltale pinwheel-revolving tail, his excited nose blowing big puffs of dust. I was only 10 yards away and clearly witnessed the explosive covey rise. There were perhaps a dozen of them, and they seemed to have Kody surrounded in whirring primaries. One pair went up from under his nose, another ducked beneath his tail making their escape, while a single brushed his flank! It was difficult to determine who was more dumbfounded, Kody or I. My confusion was more obvious, though—firing both barrels of my over-and-under did not loosen a single feather!

Those were some steely-nerved birds, but nothing out of the ordinary. I have actually approached marked birds, sitting in open ground, that have allowed me to nearly touch them with gun muzzles before they flushed.

The secret to gunning Montezuma quail with some consistency is learning to recognize suitable habitat. Montezumas could be more properly termed a mountain quail—dry mountains where grassy oak canyons and ridges and wooded slopes with healthy stands of bunch and gamma grass thrive. I have discovered Montezumas as low as 1,000 feet above sea level in southern Arizona and as high as 10,000 feet in New Mexico's Gila Wilderness and Arizona's Mogollon Rim.

Without a healthy mix of open grasslands between stands of hearty oaks, Montezumas will likely be scarce. You may also discover them in piñon and juniper forest, but without occasional patches of open grass you are probably wasting your time. If you begin to encounter a good number of cattle, it is probably best to move on in search of areas that are not being grazed. Montezuma quail and cattle are a poor mix, as the Montezuma does not tolerate grazing. Seek ridges and benches with healthy stands of grass and you will see more Montezumas.

Saucer- or teacup-sized diggings or scratching in soft earth found in the

Montezumas could be described as "mountain desert quail." Look for them at higher elevations, where grassland and oak savanna canyons mix together. These quail will venture far from water; some hunters even say they don't need standing water to survive.

Shotguns & Loads for Desert Quail

Gambel's Quail

Because it weighs only 6 pounds, I normally tote my love-worn 20 gauge side-by-side when Gambel's are on the agenda. After a day of walking under a hot sun a heavy gun becomes a burden. This double owns modified and improved cylinders, and throws high-brass, 1-ounce loads well, but does require me to pick my shots. I can remember plenty of times when I wished I had more choke constriction or my bigger 12 gauge to deal with wild flushers, but I seem to get my share with this gun. I dump No. 7½ shot into my Filson shell bag; 8s are sometimes not enough to anchor these desert-toughened birds, especially on shots past 25 yards. A wounded Gambel's is not past clambering down a rabbit hole or into mean cactus clumps that will wound your retriever.

Scaled Quail

Venturing into the realm of scaled quail weaponry proves a dicey proposition. Open or tight chokes? Twenty gauge or 12? A double of some sort, with full beside or under modified in 20 gauge, modified over improved in 12? These guns solve most dilemmas, but you may want some additional backup shots for runners. In that case a repeater with modified choke is a good compromise, but the gun becomes heavy after a long day of shank's mare, and anyway I can't make these decisions for you.

No matter the shotgun, choose No. 7½ or even 6 shot and you'll lose fewer birds; 1⅛ ounce high-brass loads in 20, or standard 1⅛-ounce in 12, are wise choices. These ain't no sissy Eastern

Here's a hat trick of desert quail—scaled, Montezuma and Gambel's, left to right, all shot on the same day. Go after them with a light shotgun that swings well, chokes tending toward the open, and No. 7½ shot.

quail! Scalies can pack some lead, and with those strong legs, a downed bird is by no means yours until in hand.

Montezuma Quail

Due to their tight-holding character, shots at Montezumas are typically point-blank and require lightening reflexes. You need to be able to hit a buzzing target at 10 to 15 yards, only occasionally farther, while at the same time avoid transforming that succulent meat into hamburger. I have the perfect Montezuma gun in my Ruger Red Label 20 gauge, with its short 26-inch barrels for fast maneuverability and skeet-over-skeet chokes for wide-open patterns. This gun makes me look good on those snap shots Montezumas ask for.

Choose light ⅞-ounce, No. 8 loads in a 20 gauge to ruin less meat, and because even on longer shots Montezumas are simply easier to ground and less prone to scooting off after only being winged. If you have a fancy 28 gauge, you might own the perfect Montezuma gun.

Like other upland hunting pursuits, chasing the desert quail gang is as much about the beauty of the place as it is the loveliness of the birds.

shade of trees, or wet spots between rock ledges, can signal that you are on track. Montezuma quail, unlike other seed-eating quail, dig for their food with oversized claws, hunting small tubers and succulent roots. It is this diet that allows the Montezuma to survive without standing water. Where you find fresh scratching, birds will be close.

Flushing a Montezuma, and swatting down a Montezuma with a load of chilled shot, do not go hand in hand. Flusher or pointer, your pooch will supply ample warning that a flush is coming, and these flushes are normally point-blank. From there it becomes more a matter of reflexes. Montezumas flush with the aid of rocket boosters, then proceed to use available vegetation to dodge your best shots.

You can't think about a Montezuma shot. You just do it. Pick a single and get on him within 10 or 15 yards or he'll

Author Patrick Meitin and Kody with the object of their affection.

put a bush or tree or cliff edge between you and him in a hurry. Shots are off the muzzles with wide-open chokes, light loads and small-gauged scatterguns. Leave the duck gun at home. Expect to prune some shubbery in the process. Clambering back off the mountain with a five-bird limit in the game pouch is something to be proud of, I can assure you.

LOVE IN THE DESERT

I admire and respect bobwhites, and shoot them whenever the chance arises. But make my quail those of the desert.

Like the land they inhabit, these denizens of the Southwest are untamed, unruly and perhaps unrefined. But I prefer my upland sport this way. Unrefined as the quail of the desert may be, and with all due respect for Gentleman Bob, they are still the most beautiful of all.

174

Finding Desert Quail

The Grand Canyon State probably offers the best all-around quail hunting in the Southwest, perhaps the nation, with southeast Arizona providing the opportunity to take a desert quail "hat trick," or three species of quail in a single day. Areas near the Chiricahua, Dragoon and Patagonia mountains are public-land areas to look to, with a good mix of National Forest, Bureau of Land Management and state lands open to hunting.

Some of the best Gambel's quail hunting in the nation is found on Arizona's two Apache Indian reservations. The San Carlos Apache Indian Reservation, near Globe, and White Mountain Apache Indian Reservation (Fort Apache), near Pinetop/Lakeside, offer a few million acres of prime quail habitat between them and very reasonable daily hunting rates of about $10. Montezumas are available in some higher-altitude areas on both. The White Mountain Apaches offer guided hunts for those who wish to hit the ground running. Contact San Carlos Recreation & Wildlife Department (520-475-2653) or the White Mountain Apache Wildlife & Outdoor Recreation Division (520-338-4385).

The Land of Enchantment's best chance for a desert quail hat trick is found in the bootheel region of the extreme southwest corner of New

A desert quail trip is definitely worth the planning time and investment. Gorgeous country and three wonderful birds to hunt make it a trip of a lifetime. But then you'll realize you can't do it just once.

Mexico. The Peloncillo and Burro mountains offer abundant populations of public-land Gambel's, occasional scaled quail, with Montezumas at higher elevations. Farther north, areas around the southern lobe of the Black Range can be extremely good for all species, though the best hunting is normally found on or through private lands where trespass fees must be arranged by knocking on ranch-house doors. The Black Range, and San Mateo Mountains farther north, offer some of the state's very best Montezuma hunting. Eastern New Mexico hot spots such as Mescalero Sands and the Caprock, east of Roswell and Artesia, offer top-drawer scalie hunting. A quality outfitter can help get you into birds.

The Lone Star State is known by many as Bobwhite Central, though scaled quail hunting can be quite good in West and South Texas. Private land hunting is the name of the game here, as public areas are extremely limited. Contact a chamber of commerce in Alpine, Fort Stockton, Midland/Odessa or Paducah to locate productive scalie territory where day-use fees can be arranged with landowners. Montezuma hunting can be found in the Big Bend area of west Texas. Limited hunting can also be found in Colorado, Utah, Nevada and California.

Chapter 17

MOUNTAIN QUAIL: HUNTING THE UNKNOWN MOUNTAINEER

BY WAYNE VAN ZWOLL

"Most interesting of all American partridges ... That he is not so regarded, is because as a lonely mountaineer he is only half known." So wrote renowned naturalist John Muir about the mountain quail in 1902. A hundred years later, we still know quite little about this bird, biggest of all the quail north of Mexico.

This is a bird of the Far West, and of some of the most murderous mountain terrain there is. It's not a wonder the mountain quail is "only half known." But he is a joy to hunt, if you have the legs and energy to go after him.

Mountain quail inhabit the steep, rugged mountains of the Far West and Northwest, from California up through Oregon and Washington, into Idaho. They are handsome, multicolored birds of rugged, high places. Be prepared to work and climb for your birds!

HUNT THE HABITAT

As with any species of upland bird, half the battle of hunting is finding the habitat where the game resides. Mountain quail hunting is no different.

As hard as they are to study, we have learned that mountain quail are migratory. This is the only quail on the continent that routinely moves from high-elevation summer range to lower winter range. In fact, its movements are much like that of mule deer, with which it shares the wildlands of the West Coast.

This bird prefers shrub vegetation in early successional stages. "Brushland" is the key word when looking for mountain quail.

Fire and logging make chapparal, redwood and piñon-juniper thickets more attractive by reducing old growth and encouraging young brush. New sprouts also mean better food for mountain quail, which are mainly vegetarian—more so than most other quail.

Mountain quail prefer brushland over other habitat types. Look for places that have been logged, burned or otherwise disturbed. Chaparral makes good mountain quail cover too.

Mixed conifer and conifer-hardwood timber, especially when interspersed with brush, also holds coveys. So do high-country aspen stands surrounded by sagebrush. Chapparal (brushlands with scrub oak, thorny brush and shrubs) is also important habitat.

BRUSH & WATER

Biologists have found that mountain quail will use boulders and fallen limbs as cover but prefer dense undergrowth, so mature forests are not favored habitat. Indeed, the birds seem more than other quail to stay in the thick brush. Mountain quail in northern California typically remain within easy reach of heavy cover comprising, on average, 45 percent shrub species. Most of it is short cover—to about 8 feet in height.

The birds also like to be near water sources. In California studies, covey traffic was heaviest within 150 yards of free water. Compared to valley (California) quail, whose range overlaps, mountain quail are more apt to use steep and forested terrain. Mountain quail roost in trees or shrubs, rarely on the ground save in captivity. Covey members often use the same tree or bush and sometimes space themselves a foot apart on the same limb, sleeping with heads tucked back.

Mountain quail have been known to thrive at summer elevations of up to 10,000 feet, but 6,000 is a common summer altitude, and they move down to winter below deep snow. These quail typically trail receding snow uphill in spring, moving on ridgelines. In the fall, migrations more commonly follow ravines down to lower elevations. The birds walk rather than fly while migrating.

HUNT THE FOOD

Knowing what mountain quail eat—and when they feed—can help you find the birds.

Depending on season and the bird's life stage, plants make up from 80 to 100 percent of a mountain quail's diet. Invertebrates (mainly insects) typically account for only 5 percent of the diet and rarely exceed 20 percent.

Eighty-five plant species have been identified in mountain quail diets. The birds eat bulbs and acorns as well as seeds, fruits and flower heads. Berries—including wild grapes, snowberries, serviceberries and others—are important food.

You'll find mountain quail near water sources, like the seep in this valley. But the birds will likely spend most of their time in the steep, surrounding terrain.

Understanding Mountain Quail

A mountain quail features a straight plume on top of his head, a blue-gray neck, chest and head, and a chestnut-colored throat patch. A handsome bird indeed!

Adult mountain quail weigh about 9 ounces. The male is slightly bigger than the female, but not enough to notice under field conditions. Males and females have similar plumage. A straight black top-knot—just two feathers!—sweeps back from a gray crown. (Valley or California quail plumes curl forward.) The male's plume is longer than the female's.

There is a distinctive chestnut throat patch, bordered by a narrow black and wider white band. The head and neck are gray, shading to olive/brown on the back. The belly is white, below chestnut sides with vertical white bars. The horizontal white or buff bar above this patch of color may be partly hidden by the wing. Black, sometimes chestnut-accented feathers below the tail make the bird appear dark as it flies away. Legs and feet are gray/buff.

Mountain quail coveys are small compared to those of other quail: 3 to 20 birds, with an average of about 9. Groups of up to 60 can be found watering together, but these large gatherings include several coveys. Coveys break up in late winter in preparation for nesting.

Depending on the area, nest-building commences in early March and can be finished in a day. Nests are typically ground depressions lined with dry grass and conifer needles. They're usually well shaded and are often built next to a steep bank or hillside. An average clutch of 10 to 12 unmarked, buff-colored eggs undergoes an incubation of about 24 days.

Hatching success depends a lot on the weather. Plentiful moisture in late winter in desert habitat boosts the odds for chick survival. Both parents commonly tend the nest, though successful hatches have been made and chicks reared by one bird. Males and females are both adept at parenting.

Predators or mountain quail chicks include rattlesnakes and the long-tailed weasel. Adults have more to fear from coyotes, bobcats, foxes and great horned owls. Accipiters—agile hawks like the goshawk and Cooper's—might account for more of these quail than any other predator.

Mountain quail range.

Mountain quail will climb into bushes and trees to reach food, and will even jump up to a foot off the ground to nip at tender leaves. Because many of the plants quail eat are hard to identify, hunters fare better looking for cover types, or dominant "indicator" plants such as bitterbrush and ceanothus.

Mountain quail forage early in the morning and late in the afternoon—good times to be out "on the edge" hunting feeding areas—but the birds commonly "snack" all day long. They drink two or three times a day, on average, and midday is a good time to hunt around watering spots. When water is scarce, they drink less often. But the birds stay near water for hours at a time when the sun is high. At dawn and dusk, water breaks are much shorter. Mountain quail will move more than a mile to reach free water.

HUNTING TECHNIQUES & TIPS

Like other quail, mountain quail flush suddenly and seem to hit top speed right away. They fly with rapid wingbeats, staying low above the cover. The birds dodge and twist into dense cover, or dive in at an angle. Chased by a hawk, mountain quail might fly straight into a thicket.

They can fly uphill, downhill or across-slope with equal skill and speed, but prefer to run uphill—even on slopes as steep as 70 degrees. On the level, they can run up to 12 mph for 100 feet or so (that's a 5-minute-mile pace!). Oddly enough, the birds use more energy walking down a hill than up—something that can't be said for hunters!

Chasing mountain quail is tough hunting, quite like what you experience going after chukars. In

Shotguns & Loads for Mountain Quail

The best shotgun for mountain quail is one that you can carry easily all day in nasty terrain. That will be a 20 gauge or a very light 12. My favorite is a Beretta Montefeltro autoloader. Ithaca's Featherlight pump, and the welter-weight Browning Citoris, are other good choices. If you have an English side-by-side that points like a wand and represents your second mortgage—leave it home. You'll fall with it on the rocks.

A modified choke prepares you for most shots. Use stiff loads of No. 6 or No. 7½ pellets. You'll want plenty in your pattern, but they must also penetrate on the long shots you'll occasionally take. Of course, any quail hunting is more sporting with a 28 gauge. You just have to discipline yourself to pass on the long shots.

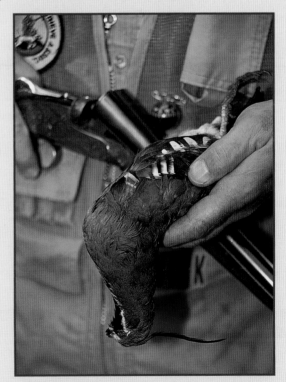

Use a light shotgun you can carry up and down all day, and a stiff load of No. 6 or 7½ shot.

the southern part of the range, dog boots are a good idea, and dogs should be snake-wise.

You'll kill more birds if you key on brush and water, two elements essential to mountain quail in the tough country they inhabit. Stout walking boots, a brimmed hat and plenty of water in your daypack are essential. If you're in good physical shape you'll cover more country and increase your chances for shooting.

Hunt across-slope, knowing that the birds like to run uphill. (Approach from below and they'll outrun you!) Come down on quail you know are there, and post a hunter below to "squeeze" them and force them to flush.

Avoid unnecessary climbing—it will tire you quickly! Zigzag along the hillsides, hitting the thickest cover. Walking a roadway is fine, if you have a dog to get into the brush and work. Send your dog up and down the steep slopes.

Always be on the lookout for birds running or sneaking away. Fire a shot their way, if you have to, to make them fly.

If you flush a covey, listen for their "assembly" calls to pinpoint birds' locations, then go after the singles or pairs.

Mountain quail like to run uphill, so hunt from the high points; never approach from below.

A DIFFERENT KIND OF HUNT

Mountain quail hunting is demanding—not at all like wagon hunts for bobwhites. Walking, climbing, busting brush—the work is hard indeed. But the Far West's high country is without match—whether you shoot a limit of the "unknown mountaineer" or not. Just a bird or two is all you need, really, out there among the grandeur of the mountains.

Finding Mountain Quail

As of this writing, mountain quail may be hunted in California from September through most of January, including the general fall bird season and a special early season for this species only. Nevada also welcomes mountain quail hunters—though its wildlife agency notes that in the southern sector of the state (and throughout the entire eastern part of its range) this bird is not doing well.

Idaho does not permit hunting of mountain quail; the species is not listed as game in Arizona, New Mexico, Utah or Colorado.

Mountain quail may be hunted west of the Cascade Range in Oregon and Washington and in four counties of eastern Oregon (Wasco, Klamath, Hood River and Wallowa). It's important that you check current regulations and be able to quickly distinguish mountain quail from other species under field conditions. The fringes of mountain quail habitat may hold lots of Valley quail.

Chapter 18

VALLEY QUAIL: COVEYS ON THE FRINGE

BY WAYNE VAN ZWOLL

lentiful now in most of its range, the valley quail (also called the California quail) is to Oregon, Washington and California what the bobwhite is to the Deep South. This is a prolific bird, quite tolerant of climatic extremes and resilient under heavy hunting pressure—which it gets!

Valley quail live in many kinds of habitat—from arid, desert-type lands to sagebrush to cool tropical forests—from the Baja Peninsula to British Columbia. They are hearty birds of tough terrain.

Birds of the fringe, valley quail (also known as California quail) reside in agricultural areas—unlike their mountain quail cousins. Valley quail are handsome birds (far left and left), resplendent in their black top plume, blue-gray coat, russet accents and scaled belly.

HUNT THE RIGHT HABITAT

Like the mountain quail, the valley quail likes brushy places interspersed with grassy fields and openings. However, this bird is more apt than the mountain quail to be found in settled areas, and often appears in suburbs and even brush lots in cities.

Valley quail inhabit the fringes of farm and orchard land, where established stands of chaparral, manzanita, sagebrush and bitterbrush provide hiding cover. These quail also occur in oak savannahs, piñon-juniper thickets and young woodlands—almost anywhere they can find low, thick, brushy cover to retreat to after using more open feeding areas. They love tangles of clematis.

While they thrive in dry country, valley quail leave severely arid sites to Gambel's quail. Valley quail range typically gets enough precipitation to ensure not only plenty of brush but a thick carpet of grasses and forbs in the openings. But heavy rainfall is hard on adults and frequently lethal to chicks. In areas of heavy snowfall,

Understanding Valley Quail

A valley (California) quail (*Callipepla californica*) is a bit more slender than a bob-white but stands about as tall. A medium-sized quail, it has a bold black chin and white bib, with a white lateral band over a buff/brown forehead. There's a brown patch on the bird's crown and nape. Six great black feathers shoot up then curl forward in a distinctive plume, thick and rounded on its front end like a question mark. The neck is speckled black and white, as if the quail were wearing chain mail. A solid gray breast becomes, abruptly, a buff-colored belly with black and beautiful "scaling." That is, the belly feathers are rimmed in black. There's a chestnut patch at the belly's center; sides are streaked brown, black and white.

Though it acts a bit like its relatives the mountain quail and Gambel's quail, and even shares some of the same habitat, the valley quail is readily distinguishable. Unlike the mountain quail, the female valley quail is not nearly as striking as her mate, and the mountain quail's plume is straight, swept back. The Gambel's quail has a forward-swooping topknot, but a longer one. It also has a brighter crown, a black belly patch (males only) and chestnut flanks. It lacks the male valley quail's black neck markings.

Except in the breeding, nesting and hatching season, valley quail forage and roost in coveys—though some research suggests that the family, not the covey, is the primary social group. Shortly after the hatch, females with young may move alone or in small groups apart from the birds they'd otherwise accompany. Coveys are larger than those of mountain quail—commonly 20 to 50 birds and sometimes as many as 70. Harsh winter weather may pull several coveys together in places where food and cover are best.

Courtship and mating occur later in the north than in the south. In much of valley quail range, birds begin laying eggs in late April but may con-

Valley quail cock (left) and hen (right).

tinue into June as successful nesters bring off a second brood. Nests or clutches that fall victim to floods or predators can be replaced by repeat matings into late summer.

The most common call of the valley quail is the assembly cry: "cu-COW-cow" or "chi-ca-go." Listen for it after you've flushed birds. Soft individual-contact putts and peeps are audible only up close. The alarm call is a series of pit-pits, given in ascending frequency as danger approaches. During mating season, unattached males yelp "cow!" to advertise their services.

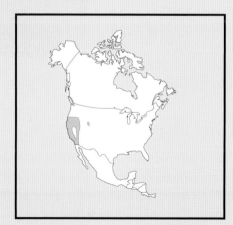

Valley quail range.

184

Look for valley quail in brushy places close to fields, pastures or other openings ... and water. The birds love to eat seeds and especially buds and berries.

shrubs and low trees.

When hunting, look for valley quail in brush next to fields, close to watering spots, in berry thickets and in dense cover along creeks.

HUNT THE FOOD & WATER

Knowing what they eat—and when they eat it—can help you find valley quail. Water is important to their lifestyle too.

Adult birds eat seeds, leaves, buds, berries, catkins and other parts from a wide variety of plants. Diets include such unlikely items as mustards and rabbitbrush. In some areas, the birds subsist largely on acorns. Legumes like alfalfa and vetch can also figure heavily in quail diets. Where available, the birds also eat grains, especially wheat. Insects typically comprise a small percentage of what a quail eats.

valley quail congregate under canopies of plants like sagebrush and wild rose. Roosting may take place on the ground or on the branches of

Shotguns & Loads for Valley Quail

The best quail gun I ever owned was a 5½-pound side-by-side, a 20-bore with a straight grip. It was quicker than a grasshopper and easy to pack up steep Washington hills. I used 1-ounce loads of 7½ shot in improved-cylinder and modified choke. That's about as good a valley quail gun combination as you will ever find.

Valley quail are properly short-range birds; you'll have more fun with a light 20 gauge or a 28 than with a 12. Remember too that quail depend primarily on dense cover to shield them from danger. If they run, it's often toward the nearest thicket. Long flushes happen, but you'll get plenty of short shooting if you learn to spot likely cover

For maximum sport and enjoyment, hunt valley quail with a light and fast-handling 20 or 28 gauge shotgun throwing an ounce of 7½ shot through an improved-cylinder barrel.

from a distance, then work toward it quietly. A dog that works close is a great asset. And bring lots of shells. Some days, you'll find more quail (and hit fewer) than you anticipated; and bag limits in good quail states are quite generous!

Hunt feeding areas early and late in the day. Valley quails' morning feeding lasts longer than their afternoon session. Midday, go to the thick stuff or to where the water is.

Mostly, valley quail forage from the ground, but they occasionally will climb to reach food.

During most of the year, quail eat twice a day, though in stormy weather they dash from cover to snack whenever there's a break in wind or precipitation. Morning is typically the longest meal, lasting, on average, one hour. The birds often finish their evening feed in half that time. When hawks or other predators are near, quail often forgo the pre-roost meal altogether.

On warm days, valley quail seek water to drink. In cool weather, and when vegetation is succulent, quail survive handily on the moisture in forage alone. Dry habitat can be greatly enhanced by water development, in the form of guzzlers and even stock tanks; the surrounding areas can offer great hunting.

Bottom line? Hunt feeding areas early and late in the day. Work thicker cover, and areas near water, during the middle portion of the day.

HUNTING TECHNIQUES & TIPS

Valley quail mostly run from danger. In fact, they'll seldom fly unless surprised or threatened by a swift predator that can out-race them to cover. Once in thick cover, quail often mill or sit tight instead of flushing or running, even if a hunter or dog crashes into the tangle in efforts to trigger a flush.

The birds seem to know they're safest in places too tight for most predators, and that they're most vulnerable when they move. The reluctance of quail to come out from under a canopy may well be due to predation by accipiters (fast hawks) like the Cooper's hawk and goshawk.

Flight is explosive and short. Sometimes quail are in the air only a few feet. If there's brush nearby, they dive in again quickly, often twisting like leaves in the wind. If the next haven is some distance away, valley quail commonly fly straight for it, rather than dodging. They alternate quick wingbeats with long glides.

Valley quail are not as fast as they look, but the quick rise and normally short flight give hunters little time to shoot. If you go after a single that lands in a small brush patch, the bird will as likely run as fly out the other side.

Sooner or later, you'll end up in the thick stuff. Wade right in and be ready.

Long seasons mean a variety of weather conditions if you're hunting valley quail in the north half of their range. Look for birds where you might look for rabbits—not only in brushlots and in bushy hedgerows around farm fields, but in patches of bitterbrush and particularly in tangles of clematis.

Ravines with good ruffed grouse habitat are good bets for valley quail. Hillsides with old sagebrush that forms protective canopies also produce birds. Because these quail eat grass seeds as well as buds and berries, grassy knobs with surrounding

brush patches hold promise.

In dry country, pivot your hunts around water—springs, stock tanks, seeps. Visit these places in midday. Watch closely for snakes, because the places quail like to water are prime spots for rattlers (which, by the way, prey on quail eggs and nestlings). Listen for quail calls just after dawn, because these birds are quite vocal.

Coveys you flush seldom travel far, so they can be flushed again—though they're apt to be in a tougher place or spread out as singles. It's a good idea to give the quail a break after two flushes, so you don't take too many or drive them from an area you might want to hunt again soon.

A dog is an asset, because downed birds can be hard to find. You'll want a pointer that works close and doesn't mind getting into brush.

Heavy snow concentrates valley quail under natural canopies, so you'll walk less for more birds. Expect birds to hold tight in deep snow.

BEAUTIFUL BIRD, BEAUTIFUL COUNTRY

Hunting valley quail is fun. They live where you'd like to be. And where the birds are plentiful, the shooting can be fast and fun indeed. Lace up those boots!

Hunt where there are grass seeds, buds and berries for quail food, and you'll find a brace of lovely birds for your own table.

Finding Valley Quail

Seven subspecies of valley (California) quail have been reported, ranging from Chile and Argentina to British Columbia—and Hawaii. In North America, the bird is most common in California, Nevada, Utah, Idaho, Oregon and Washington. Though abundant on the Baja Peninsula and California coast, it prefers the dry east side of northern Oregon and Washington.

Hunters—and dogs—love valley quail.

INDEX

E

F

G

H